GRIEF, TRANSITION, AND LOSS

CREATIVE PASTORAL CARE AND COUNSELING SERIES
Howard W. Stone, Editor

BOOKS IN THE SERIES

Crisis Counseling (revised edition)
Howard W. Stone

Integrative Family Therapy
David C. Olsen

Counseling Men
Philip L. Culbertson

Woman-Battering
Carol J. Adams

Counseling Adolescent Girls
Patricia H. Davis

Cross-Cultural Counseling
Aart M. van Beek

Creating a Healthier Church
Ronald W. Richardson

Grief, Transition, and Loss
Wayne E. Oates

When Faith Is Tested
Jeffry R. Zurheide

CREATIVE PASTORAL CARE AND COUNSELING

GRIEF, TRANSITION, AND LOSS

A PASTOR'S PRACTICAL GUIDE

WAYNE E. OATES

FORTRESS PRESS   MINNEAPOLIS

GRIEF, TRANSITION, AND LOSS
A Pastor's Practical Guide

Cover art: *Rocks at Belle-Isle Port Domois* by Claude Monet. Used by permission of the Saint Louis Art Museum.

Library of Congress Cataloging-in-Publication Data

Oates, Wayne Edward, 1917–
    Grief, transition, and loss : a pastor's practical guide / by
Wayne E. Oates.
        p.   cm. — (Creative pastoral care and counseling series)
    Rev. ed. of : Pastoral care and counseling in grief and separation.
Philadelphia : Fortress Press, © 1976.
    Includes bibliographical references.
    ISBN 0-8006-2864-0 (alk. paper)
    1. Pastoral theology. 2. Pastoral counseling. 3. Bereavement—
Religious aspects—Christianity. I. Oates, Wayne Edward, 1917–
Pastoral care and counseling in grief and separation. II. Title.
III. Series.
BV4011.023 1996
253'.5—dc21   96-49123
                                                                                 CIP

The paper used in this publication meets the minimum requirements of American National Standard for Information Sciences—Permanence of Paper for Printed Library Materials, ANSI Z329.48-1984.

Manufactured in the U. S. A.   AF 1-2864

To

Pauline

My Beloved Wife

CONTENTS

FOREWORD

In *Grief, Transition, and Loss: A Pastor's Practical Guide,* Wayne Oates has written a new, up-to-date book on subjects for which he has long been known. His previously published book in this series, *Pastoral Care and Counseling in Grief and Separation* (Fortress, 1976), has been a bestseller throughout the world. His new volume has even more wisdom, wide knowledge, and practical suggestions.

With *Grief, Transition, and Loss,* Oates helps readers recognize that what they learn from offering pastoral care to the bereaved relates to many other losses in people's lives. In the opening chapter of the book Oates describes grief and takes us along on the journey of the bereaved. The reader will soon recognize that the path has also been taken by the author, for it is written in a personal and compassionate way. The author has experienced losses and has reflected on them. He has also sympathetically helped many others with their griefs. We benefit from this reflection, for he clearly describes the process of the bereaved.

The book then deals with a variety of losses. It not only talks about the loss of a spouse or a parent; it also addresses the death of a son, daughter, or grandchild. It covers spontaneous miscarriage, abortion, suicide, the birth of a malformed child, and death by murder. It addresses the losses of bodily functions—hearing, sight, and sexuality. Chapter 4 focuses on separation and divorce—one of the most useful parts of the book. Oates sensitively describes the course that a divorce usually takes. Chapter 5 covers losses in the world of work. These work and vocation-related losses certainly have been an area where my pastoral care and counseling have expanded since the publication of the previous book. Oates's discussion of corporate downsizing, takeovers, and fired or laid-off workers is critically important to the care and counseling that many pastors face. With all the above losses, he notes how what we have learned from caring for the bereaved can help us understand these many griefs.

Grief, Transition, and Loss is a book that people will talk about decades from now. It helps us chart a course through the moiled waters of loss and pilot a way through turbulent grief.

HOWARD W. STONE

ACKNOWLEDGMENTS

I am indebted to my colleagues Henlee Barnette, Walter Jackson, and Samuel Southard for their consultations with me about this book as I formulated the thoughts presented here. While books are written when we are alone, they are, at best, developed in a community of learning. These friends have been and continue to be that community to me.

I am especially indebted to my wife, Pauline Rhodes Oates, who has been my steadfast love and companion as we have borne many griefs and separations from many people over more than a half century.

Genuine gratitude is due Dr. Marshall D. Johnson, Dr. Cynthia Thompson, and Fortress Press for encouragement and highly competent editing of this manuscript into a book.

My special and deep appreciation goes to Laura Allen, my computer specialist, who prepared this manuscript and endured my handwriting. Laura Allen came to my rescue when my computer died a natural death of old age just as I started this book.

1

CARING AT THE TIME
OF EMERGENCIES

As caregivers you and I are crisis interveners. Crises in human situations are of two kinds—developmental crises and emergency crises. Developmental crises are those that occur in the normal process of growth from birth to death, the common ventures of life that most of us share—the birth of a baby, the beginning of school, adolescence, marriage, midlife and the emptying of the nest as children grow up and leave home, retirement, nonlethal illnesses, old age, and death after a ripe old age. These all call for caregiving, much of which is *celebration*, of the birth of a baby, a wedding, a graduation, and so on.

Any one of these, however, can suddenly turn into an *emergency* crisis, such as the stillbirth of a child, abrupt cancer in a child, an emotional breakdown of a person in adolescence, a sudden death upon retirement, or accidental deaths that result from auto or plane accidents, a swimming or playground accident, and a host of other tragedies. Our evening news is filled with accounts of emergency, traumatic crises. A suicide or a homicide, the destruction of a home by fire, a murder, a sudden death by heart attack, or any of the thousand mental ills can suddenly turn a seemingly placid life situation into a horror story.

THE UNSPOKEN EXPECTATIONS
OF A CHRISTIAN CAREGIVER

We as Christian caregivers have a unique place in people's lives at the time of an emergency. After the manner of the suffering servant in Isaiah 53:3, we can be persons "of sorrows, acquainted with grief." Emer-

gency crises are almost always times of sorrow and grief. We are expected as Christians to respond by taking the initiative and intervening as
ministers of encouragement, stability, and hope.

Caregivers wonder, "What shall I *say?*" "What can I *do?*" Yet these
questions are secondary to our being a *presence*, a reminder of the Presence of God in Jesus Christ, that the sufferers are not alone. We are
sharers with them of their burdens as we fulfill the law of Christ (Gala-
tians 6:2). Our own self-awareness of this "being with" them prompts
us to give thanks that neither they nor we are alone; the Presence of
God is with us, bearing the pain, agony, and desolation with us. Jesus
told us he would not leave us desolate, literally, "as orphans," in times
of crises when severe tragedy strikes. Thus it is not what we can *say* or
do, it is what we *are*, who we can be, the kind of presence we bring to
them, whom we represent—the Lord Jesus Christ.

DETERMINING WHETHER A SITUATION IS AN EMERGENCY

One of the caregivers' greatest temptations is to consider *every* call
upon his or her services to be an emergency. We need to be needed and
it meets our needs to jump and run at every request. Thus, as Jethro,
Moses' father-in-law, told him, "We wear ourselves and our people out
and the thing will be too heavy for you. . ." (Exod. 18:18). Therefore,
we need to develop the skills of the triage, the art of separating out different degrees of emergency in the requests that come our way. Triage
is a battlefield hospital metaphor. Casualties are seen as they come in
and assessed as to the degree of emergency they are suffering. In civilian emergency rooms a triage officer is on duty at all times. He or she
sees to it that, for instance, a person suffering a heart attack will be seen
by physicians before a person with a broken arm or an infected bladder.

In our work as Christian caregivers, we are our own triage officers.
The call of the wife of a man who has disappeared after leaving a note
in his car saying that he has been kidnapped and a sales receipt for a pis-
tol in the desk drawer will certainly be judged as an emergency. But the
call of a couple about plans to be married a year from now would be
given some instructions about the wedding over the telephone and an
appointment to be seen in a month.

Common sense teaches us that life or death situations take priority over those that have no life or death implications in them. If one gets a late evening call from a couple who are debating whether to sell their house and move to another city, their concerns can be heard empathically for a ten or fifteen minute conversation, and they can be seen in the next day or even next week in their home or one's office. But a person who calls and says that her spouse has been taken by an emergency medical team to the hospital with a self-inflicted gunshot wound might require a caregiver to arise at three in the morning and go to the hospital as soon as possible to be with the family.

Common sense also teaches us that a careful evaluation of a call for help will be appreciated by a caller if the caregiver listens and asks exploratory questions. After listening carefully to the person's appeal, one may ask, "How much of an emergency is this for you?" Or "How much pressure are you under for us to sit down together and study the problem to make a good decision?" Or "Today is just about over; would you feel at ease if we met tomorrow morning?"

Such separating out different degrees of emergency is a spiritual gift of discernment in which we test the spirits of people in a compassionate and firmly gentle way. This gift of discernment comes to us from the Holy Spirit, according to 1 Cor. 12:10. Discernment is one of the gifts of the Holy Spirit "for the common good."

THREE PHASES OF EMERGENCY CAREGIVING

As we become a caring presence to persons in emergencies, we need a practical grasp of our task. It can best be seen in a threefold process. (1) The caregiver moves the situation out of panic, severe alarm, and loss of control into a calmer, steadier, and less terror-stricken state of being. (2) The caregiver mobilizes emergency assistance (loved ones and professional help) for stricken persons. If there is a death, the deceased's loved ones may be beside themselves with anxiety and overwhelmed into inaction. The situation is out of control and must be brought under control. (3) The caregiver works out plans for the longer term care of the stricken person(s) and provides spiritual support, continuing guidance, and encouragement. If the stricken one died suddenly by heart attack, accident, suicide, or murder, we are faced with a particular kind of grief—sudden traumatic grief. In such situations, the caregiver can communicate the steadfast love of God. Let us look at these three phases of the process of emergency caregiving and our possible patterns of action in each one.

Stage One: Bring the Crisis under Control

A person who has just heard that his or her spouse wants a divorce, or that a loved one has been killed in an accident, died suddenly of a heart attack, or committed suicide, or that a child has been born dead, is likely to become highly agitated, cry profusely, or even scream and say highly irrational things. People in such situations can lose control. This is not a bad thing for them to be doing. It is far better than acting as if nothing has happened or being stunned into total numbness.

Yet in all these states confusion is the disorder of the day. We as caregivers can and should do several things.

1. Go to the scene of the crisis *immediately,* as soon as you have heard of it. When you go promptly, you can say, "I came as soon as I heard. I want to be with you in this terrible time."

2. You can let the sobbing ones cry on your shoulder (while respecting personal boundaries). As you do so you can guide them from a standing position to a seat and kneel by them as you comfort them.

3. You can hear their complaints: "This is not fair." "Why has God done this to me?" They may be fiercely angry, with no one but God to take their anger. You can encourage them by saying that God can take their anger and is no doubt as angry as they are.

4. All this time, they may be talking in loud voices. You can calm them by talking in a lower, quieter voice, bringing them down to a calmer level.

5. If they faint or show symptoms of illness, you can see that a physician or paramedic team (911) is called. People have been known to die when they face a severe traumatic emergency.

6. You are a person of prayer, and the gathering of the individual and group in a time of heartfelt prayer led by you puts the whole crisis into God's hands and brings the presence of God in Jesus Christ into vivid awareness. This is probably the most calming and steadying thing you can do.

7. You can move the now calmed situation to the second phase.

Stage Two: Mobilizing the Support System of the Person

The larger family and friendship circle of the stricken ones are a major part of those who sustain and support us in times of emergency. Yet, they may need to be notified. We can get the more composed of the people there to start "notifying the next of kin" about what has happened. We may do part of this ourselves.

Then, too, other caregivers may be needed. For example, calling the physician or 911 is to call other caregivers. If we are not the pastor, we can call the person who is the pastor. If the stricken ones have not eaten for a while, by all means fluids warm and/or cold should be gotten. A supply of facial tissue for the drying of tears is needed. If necessity calls for us to leave the scene, we need to call for a replacement. A calm and steady colleague or the family member that "holds up well" can help. (Later this person needs our attention when we can pull this person aside and debrief him or her about his or her own feelings. Special friends of the stricken ones are often more supportive and helpful than the members of the extended family. We can carefully find out who they are and see to it that they are called.

At this stage, in case of a death, the preliminary arrangements for a funeral have to be made. A particular funeral home needs to be decided upon and called. The person to conduct the funeral needs to be involved as soon as possible. Planning the funeral is the first step toward this person's journey beyond this emergency to picking up the pieces of life and getting on with the rest of life. A time of prayer in the face of this pain of planning to say good-bye to the deceased is needed.

Stage Three: Planning for the Longer Term Care of the Persons Now in Crisis

A considerable number of persons huddle around most people at the first moments and days of a crisis. But it does not take long for this crowd to thin out as they go back to work and resume the routine of life. This is when a shocked, numbed, depressed victim of a crisis faces going back to work and the regular routine of life alone.

The wise caregiver knows that this leaves the victim isolated. He or she plans, therefore, to telephone the victim regularly and to assess their situation as they do so. How are they doing? Are they able to sleep enough? Are they living alone or is someone with them? We are continuing to think about them, and pray for them and are at their service. A prayer over the telephone is appropriate and gives an eternal context for the day-to-day working through of the losses or new burdens the person is experiencing. Companionship with fellow church members is an undergirding grace. The fellowship of believers incarnates the teaching of the Apostle Paul in II Cor. 1:3—"Blessed be the God and Father of our Lord Jesus Christ, the Father of mercies and the God of all consolation, who consoles us in all our affliction, so that we may be able to console those who are in any affliction with the consolation with which we ourselves are consoled by God."

THE MINISTRY OF PRAYER IN EMERGENCIES

I recall being asked by a student of mine to come immediately to the maternity ward at one of our hospitals. He simply stated, "There are three of us as fathers who are in great need of you." I learned from him that the wife of one of them had given birth to a healthy, well formed child. The wife of one of them had given birth to a child that was dead on arrival (but the mother was doing well). The wife *and* the baby of one of them had both died. What an emergency!

I went immediately to their sides. I got them in a conference room, and the first thing we did was to go to God in prayer. I started the prayer by saying. "O Lord, you told us that sufficient unto the day is the evil thereof, and we certainly have had enough calamity to last many days. O Lord, have mercy upon us as we celebrate the life of one baby that is safe and comfort us in the three heart-breaking deaths we must mourn. Amen." Then I asked each one to tell me what had happened to his wife and baby. I "debriefed" each one and enabled them to sustain one another. We made plans for the care of the bodies of the deceased and for the notification of the families of each one and for funerals of the deceased. Then we had a prayer time in which each one of us expressed his feelings to God and prayed for the others.

Prayer in times of emergency when timed accurately is the greatest gift we can share with people in their acute state of being. Then, too, it keeps us reminded that we are not alone in this ministry. The presence of the God of our Lord Jesus Christ is there with us, too.

2

THE PASTOR:
A PERSON OF SORROWS,
ACQUAINTED WITH GRIEF

In earlier translations of Isaiah 53:3 (KJV and RSV), the Suffering Servant of Israel, a prototype for Christians of the Great Shepherd, Jesus the Christ, was described as "a man of sorrows, and acquainted with grief." Pastors today are undershepherds of Jesus the Christ. Our task as pastors is to be, as he was, a person of sorrows acquainted with grief.

This role defines our ministry to those suffering from grief and separation. To say that we are persons of sorrows infers that we ourselves have suffered losses and separations. Accordingly, we have been obliged to explore our own experiences with grief and separation. Yet our own losses and estrangements are *our* sorrows; we do not burden people we are serving with our stories. Their accounts of their griefs and separations prompt us instead to revisit our own histories and disentangle them from the stories of the people we serve. Their suffering is *like* but not *the same* as ours. Thus they throw light on our histories of suffering. Our histories create an empathy for them. Nonverbally people cared for sense that you and I are fellow sufferers. We are acquainted with sorrows. We are no strangers to grief.

This slow wisdom of grief prevents repetition of the clichés of people who have never suffered grief and separation. For example, we do not say to a couple who have lost a child that they can have another child and that this possibility should comfort them. Nor do we say to a widow of a military casualty that she has her youth and can find a replacement husband. Such clichés are common and come as cold comfort to a grieving person. Our task, by contrast, it to facilitate the person's telling his or her own story of grief and or separation. If persons can put into words the nameless feelings that overwhelm, they

become wiser in their prayers and are better equipped to turn their
tears and unutterable sorrow into meaningful words. Yet the people
around the bereaved, divorced, and estranged tend to skirt such conversation by avoiding talking about the losses the person is suffering,
by changing the subject. The person of sorrows, however, faces the
issue of grief head-on and enables the grieving persons to "talk out"
their sorrow.

THE GIFT OF DISCERNMENT

As we approach the task of caring for the bereaved, we can best pray for
the gift of discernment of spirits to understand the bereaved and/or
separated persons to whom we are called to minister. With discernment, the pastor can more effectively "bind up the broken hearted"
(Isaiah 61:1). For, as Proverbs 20:5 says, "The purposes in the human
mind are like deep water, but the intelligent will draw them out." A
person of such understanding today can combine the wisdom of the
Word of God with the wisdom of present-day research to benefit the
broken hearted. Several bodies of data can be used in this ministry.
They are as follows.

Different Kinds of Grief and Separation

Not all grief and separation are alike by any means. A pastor is most
effective when he or she discerns the different kinds of grief. Forms of
grief call for diagnosis, meaning, and treatment. In our research and
service we have isolated and will describe at least six quantitatively different kinds of grief: anticipatory grief, acute or sudden grief, chronic
sorrow, "Near miss" grief, pathological grief, and the sense of life. I will
discuss each of these briefly.[1]

1. Anticipatory grief is a double grief, the grief of a person dying
with a long-term grief over his or her gradual loss of life due to a ter-
minal illness such as cancer and the grief of the family and close
friends of the dying person. The patient goes through the process formulated by Elizabeth Kübler-Ross. I have seen dying patients who did
not go through the process but fought death in mortal combat until
the last breath was drawn. Robert Browning describes this in his
poem *Prospice*.

I was ever a fighter, so—one fight more,
The best and the last!
I would hate that death bandage my eyes, and forebore,
And bade me creep past.[2]

Such variations of the anticipation of death make each person's
dying unique and idiosyncratic, defying a neat process of any kind.
The community grieving with the dying person has its own crisis of
grief to endure over a time that itself varies from patient to patient.
These crises have been mentioned in the previous chapter. Each crisis,
from diagnosis to the return to the resumption of work and the regular routine of life, is a ritual in its own right experienced idiosyncrati-
cally by each family. The differences emerge from the unique style of
relationship within each family.

2. Sudden or traumatic grief comes with little or no warning.
Death comes in a sudden, unexpected heart attack, an accident, a suicide, murder, or some other tragedy. A sudden divorce bursts into
being after a long, silent period of incubation. The bereaved react
with severe shock, alarm, disbelief, panic. In shock, the bereaved may
hasten back into hyperactive work, almost as if nothing has happened.
Grief work may be delayed over a longer period of time. Sadly, sudden death may cause the survivor to be more likely to grieve alone. A
pastor can do much about this possibility by his or her own personal
action and by mobilizing members of the church to provide a community of concern for the bereaved. Finally, persons suffering a sudden loss are more likely to become pathologically bereaved than is the
person suffering anticipatory grief. The latter grieves in "install-
ments" over a preparatory period of time. A sudden bereavement
comes more as "a thief in the night" and has more damaging physi-
ological as well as psychological affects.

3. Chronic sorrow or "no end" grief is dramatically different from
anticipatory and sudden grief. Chronic sorrow can mean living with a
badly deformed or retarded child, caring for a spouse with
Alzheimer's, being the family member of a loved one serving a life sen-
tence in prison, or any "no end" grief of this sort. This kind of grief
could as well be called "the death of a dream." The dream was for a

healthy, well-formed child, being capable of enjoying retirement together (as in the case of the spouse of someone with Alzheimer's) and of serving a loved one who is crime free, free of substance abuse, and one who is a law-abiding, hardworking success in a productive job (as in the case of the life term in prison). These conditions go on and on and on. The caretaker says, "There is no end to this." Hence, I have taken the sufferer's own words to name chronic sorrow "no end" grief.

Being a pastor to such persons and families is being in the pilgrimage with them "for the duration." If you should change pastorates, you would, with the family's permission, want to inform your successor and a trusted lay person of their situation.

Ministry to them consists of their periodically briefing you, your debriefing them and asking God for the *endurance* to live their life a day at a time, asking for strength each day. The prayer of Reinhold Niebuhr is appropriate:

> Lord, grant me the serenity to accept the things
> I cannot change
> The courage to change the things
> that I can change
> And the wisdom to know the difference.

Since 1980, the whole world has been besieged by the human immune virus that progresses into the killer disease of the autoimmune deficiency AIDS. The time between being diagnosed HIV positive and the time the person dies of AIDS varies widely from one individual to another. This is not a specific no end grief but a long, chronic sorrow. On the day this is being written, a "CBS Sixty Minutes" segment portrayed a man in the earlier stages of HIV providing assisted suicide for eight AIDS patients before dying of AIDS himself.

The pastoral care of AIDS patients and their families calls for education about how the disease is and is not contracted, that shaking hands, hugging, or laying hands on the patient's brow or shoulder do *not* transmit the disease. Educating the family is another pastoral challenge. The long, painful course of the illness is a chronic sorrow for patient, family, and friends.

The Department of Psychiatry at the University of Louisville School of Medicine has had a federal grant for AIDS education in our community. The churches are focal institutions for this program. Prayers for the cure of this disease must be added to education in coping over the months and years of this sorrow.

4. "Near miss" grief is the kind in which a person narrowly escaped being killed, as in the case of the combat soldier who barely missed death when fellow soldiers were killed. Such cases, involve "survivor guilt." Consider the example of Charles Bugg and his family, whose son suffered cancer of the pineal gland. The son had surgery twice. He was ten years old in 1983 when the two cancers struck him. In addition to surgeries, he had radiation therapy. He is alive and well now in 1994. He has survived eleven years. His growth is stunted, and he takes medication for seizures. Charles Bugg has told this story in his book, *Learning to Dream Again*.[3] He speaks of grief in life, grace through life, the gift of life, and especially perseverance and gratitude for life.

I became acquainted with a near miss death when I was eight years old. Waiting for a train I stood on one of two sets of train tracks. I happened to turn my head to the left and saw another train bearing down on me. I jumped off the tracks to safety just in time. That was sixty-nine years ago, but I still think of it when at a railroad crossing. Never sit, stand, or park on a railroad track! It was a near miss, a close encounter with death.

5. Pathological grief is discerned in several ways. The most obvious one is to note how bizarre the grieving is. I think of a father whose twenty-six-year-old son was killed in an automobile accident. In the hospital emergency room, the father asked that his body be "stuffed" the way a taxidermist would do a bird or an animal. When told that this was impossible, he had his son embalmed, placed in a casket sealed as tight as possible with a glass cover on it so that his body could be seen. The casket was placed in an air conditioned room in his home. He began inviting ministers to come by and lead worship services. That is bizarre!

A colleague of mine at the University of Louisville Department of Psychiatry, Clifford Kuhn, M.D., says, "Suddenly bereaved persons are at risk for accidents, illness, or even death. Their immunological systems break down. Even cancer itself is thought to be related to such failures of the immunological systems."

Pathological grief can occur when the shock of sudden death unhinges the judgment and behavior of a severely shocked family member. For example, a thirty-five-year-old repairman dropped dead with a coronary heart attack. His coronary arteries were congenitally too small. His wife, after the funeral was over and the crowd of comforters thinned out, began going to his grave every night after her two pre-adolescent children were asleep. She expected Jesus to raise him from the dead and went to meet him. When this did not happen, she became suicidally depressed and had to be hospitalized. Here again the severity of the shock produced a pathological grief.

A religious form of pathological grief is an intense desire to be near God but complicated by the complaint that God does not care, does not hear, or does not exist. A ten-year-old girl came home from school and found the dead body of her father, who had committed suicide. She developed rituals of undoing the tragic loss of her father that were intense efforts toward reunion with her father. One was the obsession to do everything she did several times, such as when dressing to put each piece of clothing on take it off, and put it on again.

Pathological grief most often follows the long-term personality a person has exhibited long before, during, and after the loss of someone by death, by divorce, or a trauma such as the burning of a home by fire or the loss of a job. The dependent person will respond with helplessness, the antisocial person will tend to act out rage and try to manipulate God or other persons, the borderline personality will make repeated attempts at suicide and need periodic hospitalizations.

The pastoral care of the pathologically bereaved should be a collaborative effort with a trusted physician-psychiatrist. Suicidal attempts, multiple personality disorders, and the need for hospitalizations show the importance of collaboration with a psychiatrist. Sole responsibility for care of these extreme pathological states by a pastor or pastoral counselor opens him or her to the possibility of malpractice litigation. This liability was dramatically exemplified in the Nally case against the pastors of a church in California, when a young adult under their care committed suicide. They had failed to seek psychiatric consultation or referral.

When a pastor works with a psychiatrist, he or she focuses primarily on spiritual guidance, the questions of faith the person expresses, and mobilizing the fellowship of the church to prevent spiritual isolation of the person. The psychiatrist focuses on the biochemistry and safety of the person.

6. The tragic sense of life expresses the kind of grief that arises from the sense of being limited in our care of others and the sense of being subject to death ourselves.

The tragic sense of life is intensely present in pastors, physicians, nurses, emergency medical teams. For us, the tragic sense of life comes with the territory of the work we do. Wordsworth calls this poignant and wistful awareness of the mystery of human suffering "the still sad music of humanity." So much of human suffering lies in the waste of human life. When I see a poverty-stricken mother quarreling with her sixteen-year-old daughter, demanding that the daughter get an abortion or never come back home, I feel this tragic sense of life.

Such tragic sense came to me intensely when I cared for a young mother who brought her *second* badly malformed child dead on arrival into the emergency room. As I traveled home, I knew what I felt could not be put into words; I could only point at it. In such awareness, the scriptural promise is one guide to sanity: "Likewise the Spirit helps us in our weakness; for we do not know how to pray as we ought, but that very Spirit intercedes with sighs too deep for words. And God, who searches the heart, knows what is the mind of the Spirit, because the Spirit intercedes for the saints according to the will of God" (Rom. 8:26-27).

Another resource for renewal in the face of the tragic sense of life is the fellowship we have with other professionals. We can form an intimate network with fellow professionals. If they share faith in God with us together we "bear one another's burdens and fulfill the law of Christ" (Gal. 6:2).

A very present temptation of the professional caregiver is to become isolated, cut off from family and friends. If we yield to this temptation, we begin to feel sorry for ourselves and may fall into the trap of seeking sympathy from one person—often of the opposite sex—and that relationship may easily turn into an extramarital affair. We can become isolated from our family and colleagues, and such separation leads to unnecessary grief.

The outline of these six forms of grief may help to discern the uniqueness of each person's brokenheartedness. Recognizing these enables us to empathize with people who have suffered loss. Yet at the same time, paying attention to the particular grief gives objectivity to our care that comes across to the bereaved as strength and wisdom.

RESOURCES FOR CARING FOR THE BEREAVED

Specific modes of caregiving can afford us as pastors security and certainty, because we become more secure and follow a deliberately chosen mode of caring. Five such modes are demonstrated in the following story of the individual's and family's grief at the time of a death: (1) planning the funeral, (2) the funeral itself, (3) eliciting the family story of the death, (4) developing "'The Story' of a Death," and (5) the follow-up of the care. The ritual of the funeral, building a sustaining support system after the crowd of comforters has thinned out, follow-up at anniversaries, holidays, and other stressful events are the substance of postcrisis care.

1. Planning the funeral is itself an opportunity to enable the whole family to begin assimilating the reality of the death of their family member. The best way to do this is to arrange a time when you can meet the whole family, including children who are able to talk. At this time, you can "go around the circle," allowing each member to tell what he or she thinks has happened to their family member and what he or she remembers most about them. The objective is to enable them to put into words their ideas, feelings, and memories of the deceased.

After you have done this, the funeral plans can be put together. Family members can recall scriptures, hymns, and specific wishes the deceased may have expressed about the funeral. If you recall any wishes the person expressed to you, you can make these known to the family. A notebook for making notes on all this conversation provides you with the material from which you can arrange the funeral service. Anecdotes, some of which may be tender, some humorous, some religious can be woven into the plan.

The deceased may have wanted some close friend or mentor to "say a few words." Such persons should be contacted and included. Even if the deceased did not express this wish, the family may. Other persons may be able to participate to read the scripture, to have a pastoral prayer, or to give a eulogy. If you or I happen to be that person, it is proper and courteous to contact the pastor or the officiating person. It is even more correct for the pastor or officiating person to contact us. If we, as former pastor-friend, are asked to conduct a funeral, the family should be told that their pastor—if they have a pastor—should be the principal leader of the funeral and should call and invite us to assist. If there is no pastor, the person the family asks need not be concerned about this delicate situation with another pastor. A "turf" problem exists here. Awareness of the possibility of invading another pastor's turf is very important and calls for us to tread softly here.

2. The funeral itself is a time of mourning and a time of celebration of the life of the deceased with the accent on the celebration. More than that, a funeral is a time of worship of God in Jesus Christ. Thanksgiving for the ever-present help of God, the Father of our Lord Jesus Christ, is a larger factor in this worship and may be a reflection of the deceased's wish at one and the same time.

The funeral is primarily for the comfort of the family and for declaring the solidarity of the rest of the community of worshipers with the family in their grief. It is not a time for admonitions about the need of persons to "straighten up and fly right" or to convert them with the threat of death. The primary goal of the funeral is to worship God in the valley of the shadow of death and to care for the mourners.

3. Eliciting the family story of the death: The tendency for us as pastors to let families fend for themselves after the funeral is all too common. After all, there are other funerals to conduct, weddings to perform, and sermons to prepare and preach, to say nothing about hospital visitation and administrative tasks to perform. How can this be managed while caring for the family whose loved one was buried a month ago? At the time of the planning of the funeral with the whole family present, you could set a time a month ahead for another family gathering to allow you to comfort and guide them after "the crowd has thinned out."

At such a meeting of those family members who still are present in the home area, you can encourage them to talk freely about what people have said to them and how they felt. For example, clichés often offend the bereaved. One person said: "I felt very alone because no one knew how I felt, and my teacher told the other kids not to talk to me about my sister's death—(they told me she said not to mention it)." Another school child said, "Many children avoided contact with me and treated me differently, as they didn't know how I would react at a given time."[4] For a young person to put this into words at a family gathering led by the pastor is a healing grace. Reports also of "cold comfort" given also can be expressed. For example, a family who is told after the death of a very young child in a Sudden Infant Death Syndrome (SIDS) that they should not grieve too much because they can have another baby soon is cold comfort—and bad advice.

4. Developing "'The Story' of a Death": A month after a funeral the comforters have reached the point when they do not know what to say. As pastors acquainted with grief, we are interested in how the mourners feel and in enabling them to say what they feel. For example, family members at such a meeting can be asked whether they have been able to sleep and what kind of dreams they have had. Furthermore, they can be encouraged to talk about the deceased. Well-wishers tend deliberately to avoid discussing the deceased. A pastor can deliberately set an example to a family by expressing some of his own memories of the dead loved one: "I recall how he would often drink coffee with me at the nearby café. He always had a good joke or story to share with me. Many of his stories were about people in trouble and how we could help them." Then, the rhyme and reason of "putting into words" each person's parts of the family's experiences are explained. This meeting is a place where they will be heard and appreciated. Each person in the family can be encouraged to discuss "how the person died, details about the circumstances of the death, and the experience of each family member at the death or when and how each member learned of the death. A pastor is not a passive listener. He or she asks questions to enable family members to construct the story of the death. This recounting enables them to sense how the others feel. Sometimes tears or numbness may leave a person without words.[5]

The functions of such an approach are to bring emotional relief, to search for meaning, bring people together, and especially to enable children to be included in the process. "In the interests of protecting children, adults often avoid talking to them about death. . . . When children are not told "The Story," they tend to create false or inaccurate stories to explain what is happening in their family."[6]

We can understand the importance of the family story being shared when we think of the way the holocaust and the Vietnam war have been excluded from public discourse. "These events have parallels at the family level in incest, suicide, and murder."[7] Emotional relief is not possible without a sharing of the trauma of death.

5. The follow-up: The most neglected ritual in the care of the bereaved is the follow-up over the ensuing months after the loss. The first Thanksgiving, Christmas, and Easter are focal times for follow-up. The absence of the deceased loved one at these times is very painful. Especially difficult are these events if the loved one died in an accident, a suicide, or a homicide. For example, one man killed himself with a shotgun in front of the Christmas tree! He branded Christmas with the horror of his death in the minds of his family.

A visit, a telephone call, or a hand-written letter to the survivors on Thanksgiving or Christmas in the first year are effective ways of follow-up. Serendipitous contacts provide opportunities for encouragement of the bereaved. Especially important is the first anniversary of the death of a loved one.

These follow-up ministries do not all have to be done by the pastor. A pastoral care team of lay persons who have demonstrated the right interest and aptitude for the ministry can be formed to do some of the follow-up ministry. They will need to be coached by the pastor to synchronize their efforts wisely.

EVENTS THAT OCCUR IN THE FIRST YEAR

Issues arising from the following typical events may come to your attention. Or, inasmuch as you know that these events routinely occur, and if your relationship to the surviving relative is positive, you can inquire tactfully about such matters.

1. The division of the material goods and money. The written will of the deceased takes precedence in this activity. The wealthier the person was—and still is—the more complex the division will be. If the will is contested legally, the administrator of the estate will need your attention. This task is a unique grief in its own right, and the legal push and pull can take months and years. One widow endured severe sorrow when her husband's will was contested by a distant cousin. The only way the struggle was resolved was to settle the matter out of court. Instructions had been given to the widow by her husband prior to his death.

2. The living conditions of the survivor. The survivor is usually a spouse. In the case of a single parent, his or her children must be cared for by someone. This situation can be an occasion for conflict between

coattending extended family members—grandparents, uncles and aunts, and others. One of the first impulses of surviving spouses is to uproot themselves, sell their homes, and move to "the old home place" near brothers and sisters or grown sons or daughters. A widower was brought to my city by his daughter and her husband, both of whom were busy physicians. He knew no one here except them, although he was well-cared for otherwise in living with them. Very soon, isolation, boredom, and time on his hands pushed him into clinical depression that required hospitalization. He finally was able to say that he wanted to return to his own home territory, where he had friends, was active in his church, and was known and loved by the whole small town. The daughter and her husband agreed to help him move on the condition that he had a housekeeper. Then, too, who knows but that he had his eye on a widow or a never-married single woman in that small town?

3. *Breaking up housekeeping.* This is an additional grief for a person who has recently lost a spouse. Fortunately, the daughter mentioned above had left the home place as it was and not sold it or its furnishings. She anticipated that the first move would be experimental. Others, however, too quickly want to sell their houses and move. You as a pastor can encourage them not to stack one grief upon another by breaking up housekeeping. The familiar belongings, such as pictures, things that were given to them by the deceased spouse, even toys of now grown children, and so on, provide reminiscences that are healing if not made into little fetishes. If the person is in excellent physical health, independent living can best be sustained with close attention by grown children.

Yet, when health, level of awareness, and capacity to function alone deteriorate, moving to a retirement home, an intermediate care center, or a skilled nursing home can be alternatives often considered today. In a rural setting, moving in with relatives often was more common than these urban possibilities. Even today living with relatives is frequent in families that do not have money to pay for retirement homes and nursing homes.

4. *The search for fellow sufferers.* Churches and communities are increasingly providing groups for sufferers of losses by death. Widows' groups seem the most prevalent. Therapeutically, these groups empha-

size healing of the pain of losses through members' sharing with one another. The more experienced mourners comfort the most recently widowed. The formation of such groups of widowers is not nearly so common. It may be that men remarry more quickly, but the lack of statistical data means that this idea is a hunch that needs research. Occasionally one sees a widow and widower find each other after having been great friends or even lovers in high school or college. Suffice it to say that suffering people tend to reach for other sufferers.

Such is true not only of spouses who have lost a mate, but also true of parents who have lost a child and of families who have lost a member by suicide. Compassionate Friends is a nationwide grouping of parents who have lost a child. SIDS groups are fellowships of parents who have lost a child by Sudden Infant Death Syndrome. S.O.S. is a group of survivors of suicide who meet regularly with professional guidance. Often such groups are organized by mental health professionals who give them continuing leadership as a part of the comprehensive mental health programs all over the country.

If you are in a larger city, Compassionate Friends can be contacted by consulting your telephone book. SIDS groups and S.O.S. can be contacted by calling your nearest comprehensive mental health centers which are government supported agencies.

GRIEF MINISTRY: A SPIRITUAL PILGRIMAGE

As we participate in the life of bereaved persons in a spiritual pilgrimage, all of us are "travelers between life and death," as Wordsworth put it. We are fellow pilgrims on this journey. Second Corinthians 1:3-4 describes this pilgrimage well: "Blessed be the God and Father of our Lord Jesus Christ, the Father of mercies and the God of all consolation, who consoles us in all our affliction, so that we may be able to console those who are in any affliction with the consolation with which we ourselves are consoled by God." The bereaved person is being consoled so that he or she "may be able" to console others who are suffering. This ministry is more than a therapeutic effort to bring persons to an adequate resolution of their grief. It is an *equipping* of them to reinvest themselves in the care of other persons in grief. For example, widows in the New Testament were divided into two groups: those who were sixty years of age or older and those younger and of childbearing age.

The first group were called "really widows" or widows indeed (1 Tim. 5:1-8), and early Christianity singled them out as recipients of social welfare, establishing an organized means of caring for the group. In the Jerusalem church a food distribution program is specified (Acts 6:1).[8] Younger widows were instructed to marry, bear children, and reinvest their lives in a family. They were encouraged not to be "idle, gadding about from house to house; and they are not merely idle, but gossips and busy bodies, saying what they should not say" (1 Tim. 5:13). They were instructed to help relatives who were "really widows" so that the church would not be burdened (1 Tim. 5:16).

The early Christians knew that grief is best managed by reinvesting life in ministry to others. Grief must not become a lifetime vocation. The consolation of others empowers us for that ministry of consolation to others.

3

GRIEF AND SEPARATION
IN THE LIFE CYCLE

Grief and separation go with us through the stages of the life cycle from birth to death. We are always finding a place and separating from a place in the transitions of our lives in relation to our community of trust, confidence, love, and faith.

BIRTH

Both an ancient, Plato, and more modern persons have perceived the experience of birth as the defining separation of our lives. Plato believed in the preexistence of the human spirit in the realm of ultimate ideas and knowledge. As we are born we pass through the waters of Lethe or forgetfulness. The rest of life consists of learning through remembering again what we knew before we were born.

William Wordsworth (1770–1850) relies on Plato in his *Ode: Intimations of Immortality*:

> Our birth is but a sleep and forgetting
> The soul rises with us, our life's star,
> Had elsewhere its setting
> and cometh from afar
> Not in entire forgetfulness
> And not in utter nakedness.
> But trailing clouds of glory do we come
> From God who is our home.[1]

The Old and New Testaments do not accent this dualism of body and soul. Biblical teaching emphasizes the wholeness of the person in community before God or isolated from the community and God. The closest we come to the idea of the wisdom of a little child is in Jesus' teaching in Matt. 18:3-5, "Unless you change and become like children, you will never enter the kingdom of heaven. Whoever becomes humble like this child is the greatest in the kingdom of heaven. Whoever welcomes one such child in my name welcomes me."

An early psychoanalyst Otto Rank speaks of birth as our first trauma, our first separation. In a very sudden event we are separated from our mother. This is the original source of anxiety, he says: "The fear in birth, which we have designated as the fear of life, seems to me actually the fear of having to live as an isolated individual. . . ." He calls the primary "fear of separation" from the whole, therefore, a fear of existing as an individual, which I should like to call the fear of life.[2] Rank, quite unintentionally, observed in the treatment of patients that often the patient "repeats, biologically, as it were, his own birth for the most part in all its details. The analysis finally turns out to be a belated accomplishment of the incompleted mastery of the birth trauma."[3]

Rank's assessment of the continuing power of fear after birth underscores the importance of the mother-father care of a newborn infant. It seems that the parents' great responsibility in the first two years of a child's life is to provide security, love, and hope for the infant. Erik Erikson, in his developmental understanding of the healthy personality, says that the earliest stage of our lives must build a foundation of *basic trust*. The lack of it is expressed in adulthood as *basic mistrust*. Erikson asserts that rudimentary *hopefulness* about life is bred in these first two years, that is, the confidence in the trustworthiness of life, the capacity to tolerate separation, and to bear up under grief.[4]

I think that we are at our healthiest when we are *in training* to face separation and death from the time we are born to the time a pet dies or is killed by a car to the stages in which we leave home to the time a family member dies. These experiences are a part of our training in grief and separation. In this training God comforts us so that we may be able to comfort other people in their time of affliction (2 Cor. 1:3–7).

Grief and separation at birth are resolved when we make peace with the mortality present in us from birth.

CHILDHOOD

Children from the time they learn to talk until adolescence experience grief very concretely. Yet when faced with the death of a parent, a grandparent, or a sibling, they are bombarded with abstractions and repressions by the adult bereavement community around them. James Agee, in his novel *A Death in the Family*—perhaps autobiographical—gives an accurate description of the abstractions and repressions about grief in two children, Rufus, who is six, and Calberine, four. Their father was killed instantly in a car accident. Their mother awakened them and sought to break the news of their father's death with them.

She told them he would not be home again because he had gone to heaven and would not be back ever again; that he got hurt and "God let him go to sleep and took him with him to heaven." Then Rufus, the six-year-old asked, "Is Daddy dead?" His mother answered finally, "Yes." She said that neither of them would understand for a while because it was so hard to understand. Rufus said to himself, "I do. . . . He's dead." It is remarkable how the six-year-old Rufus broke through his severely grieved mother's abstractions to the concrete fact that his father was dead.[5]

Another concern children face in the presence of death is the heavy load of responsibility for taking care of the surviving parent—usually the mother—in her grief. The grief of the child himself or herself is ignored. Helen Rosen quotes a woman who was a child when her brother was killed in World War II:

> I felt extreme loss that no one else seemed to understand. The relatives paid all the attention to my folks, and the one thing I resented most of all was the "Be strong for her" messages I got. People only saw the death of her son, not my brother.[6]

In the pastoral care of bereaved children, this vignette underscores the importance of affirming the child's own grief in terms of himself or herself alone, without loading the care of the adults upon them and ignoring their own feelings. Similarly, it is especially important to be quite factual and concrete and avoid pious abstractions.

For example, even adults deal in vague euphemisms about death. Many of them avoid the use of the words dead or death. They say such things as, "He's gone to a much better place"; "She has passed away"; "God needs her more than we did"; "He has gone on to his reward"; and so on. Especially in speaking to a child, these vague sayings are pure confusion. It would be better to say, "I am sad with you that your father has died." The child may ask, "What do you mean 'He has died'?" My response usually is: "He will not *move* again. Life is moving, as you move your arm, leg, or eyes. You breathe. Your daddy will never move or breathe again. His heart has stopped beating. When this happens we say that a person is dead. Now we have a funeral to thank God for your daddy, that he and his mother helped you to be born, and to thank God for you and your brother and sister. Then we bury him in the ground. His body will gradually become a part of the earth. His spirit will live on as you and your brothers and will be cared for and loved by God in God's own way. God is your friend and comforter when you are sad and lonely about your father's death. I will be your friend and you can ask me questions."

You may want to revise this to fit your own way of communication, but the essentials are to be down-to-earth, factual, and compassionate in forming a friendship with the child. Much of this can be begun at the family gathering for planning the funeral.

ADOLESCENCE

Adolescence, it can be said, is in itself a time of grief and separation.[7] Parents are no longer on their pedestals of perfection, idealization, and omnipotence, if they have not some time ago lost this deification through abuse or abandonment. My father abandoned us shortly after I was born. I never saw him but once for certain. The other time I think was a childhood fantasy, in which he came and took me to ride in a car and told me he loved me. Yet I always hoped that he would return and that our home would be less poverty-stricken and everyone would be happier. He committed suicide when I was an adolescent, seventeen, just after I finished high school. The evening after I heard of his death, I dreamed that I had died and was being buried with him. I awoke and realized immediately that it was not I who died, but my dream and hope for his return was dead and being buried with him!

Two years after that I started college and met a professor and a male pastor who became my mentors. Only recently the pastor, William Lynch, died, and the professor celebrated his eighty-sixth birthday a few days ago. I am still in touch with the professor, O. T. Binkley. Later, in my seminary days, Gaines S. Dobbins, my doctoral supervisor, became a spiritual father to me; he never treated me as a child but as a grown son. I never had a negative encounter with any one of these three men. They were steadfast as could be and reacted with wisdom, patience, and a strong sense of humor to my growing up as a late adolescent and young adult. They taught me the art of forming and maintaining mutual friendships that death itself can bereave but never destroy.

There is much that a pastor or teacher can *be* to an adolescent, especially one who has had his or her dreams and hopes in parents crashed either by abandonment, or separation, or by death, or all three.

Adolescence and Divorce

Divorce is endured by some adolescents with reasonable stability. Observation of many children of divorce prompts me to identify some variables that make for this stability in the adolescent. First, the degree of civility between the parents in the divorce process makes the transition more bearable for children. The presence of uncontrolled rage, character assassination, or brutality in physical violence destabilizes children. Second, the peaceful access of the children to both parents after the divorce makes stability more certain. Third, stability is increased if the children are faithfully supported financially by both parents. Divorce can dissolve a marriage but should not destabilize the children; they are the one flesh personified. Fourth, grandparents can be either a positive or a negative factor. In this highly mobile society, geographical distance makes contact between generations difficult. In my own history, my maternal grandmother was with us from my birth until her death, which occurred when I was twenty. She made all the difference for me.

But what happens to adolescents who have major difficulty after the parents divorce? I have observed children before, during, and after divorce. Some adolescents who were previously very talkative and spontaneous become guarded and minimal in their conversation with adults. To hear them speak with their friends on the telephone, this is not true of their situation with peers. Second, money often becomes scarcer, and these teenagers may manipulate other adults in the family for money. At worst, they may steal from relatives. These two behaviors seem to me to be rooted in basic distrust of adults. They are closed in and do not risk having what they say get back to one or the other parent. They mourn within themselves and look out for their own survival.

When adolescents lose a very close friend, especially a friend of the opposite sex with whom they are in love, they find difficulty in being recognized as broken-hearted. Rosen tells of a sixteen-year-old boy whose girlfriend was killed in a biking accident. The parents and relatives would not let him come in their houses nor attend her funeral. His own parents were somewhat glad that he could "spend more time with his studies." "He had to find out about the accident at school; no adults to tell him. He was numb, disbelieving, angry, and depressed. No one comforted him. He was especially afraid to show his grief and tears to his schoolmates lest they think he was a sissy."[7] Such exclusion can lead to depression or acting-out disorders. In late adolescence, alcohol or other drugs may set youth up for adult vulnerability.

Youth groups at church may function as support groups for adolescents who are bereaved. Larger churches might have youth ministers on their staff. Yet this task should not be completely delegated to a staff member. The senior pastor can be especially helpful by making some effort to include the adolescents in the grieving community. He or she can provide individual times of conversation with the most intimate friends of the deceased. By all means, he or she must not join other adults in being covertly amused and taking lightly the adolescents' grief over the friend's death.

More recently public and private school counselors and teachers have begun holding debriefing sessions for the whole peer group of a deceased comrade. Youths are encouraged to put their deepest feelings into words and not to suffer in isolation and silence. Pastors can provide a similar opportunity at church.

LOSSES IN ADULT LIFE

The major losses in adulthood are the death of a parent, a spouse, or a child. The loss of parents is a severe loss, especially when it is a premature death. Today, adults in their fifties, sixties, and seventies are losing parents who are in their seventies, eighties, nineties, and even hundreds. These deaths often occur after long debilitating illnesses, prominent among which is Alzheimer's disease. I have just returned from the funeral of a ninety-year-old mother of a close friend who has spent four years in caring for her. The relief this daughter feels mingles in a bittersweet way with her loss of her mother. Her father is long since dead. It is a blow to become an orphan at any age.

Rev. Linda Stack Morgan is a Methodist pastor at Ansonville, North Carolina. I recently had the privilege of reading an Easter sermon that she delivered on April 3, 1994. She tells of the death of her father in 1990. He died of a brain tumor at the age of sixty-eight after an illness of six months. Three years after his death she had dreamed the following dream, which she permits me to report to you:

> In the dream, I was in the eating area of a home. My dad entered from an outside door. He looked completely well. In fact, he looked more well than I ever remember having seen him on earth. He seemed very centered. His demeanor was that of straightforward integrity. There were no signs of inner pain from experiences in the war. There were no signs of illness from brain tumors or the radiation that tried to beat them back. My dad seemed complete as a person, whole, serene. He did not appear to have a need to call to me or to beckon me in any way. A woman entered the dream. She placed a meal in front of my dad. He began to eat with obvious gratitude and serenity in his face.

"I awoke from the dream. Out of it I felt a deep sense of calm. . . . He was in a state of consideration fleshed out in the full humanness of the truth of God."

After three years her grief over the loss of her father was resolved in this dream. She was reinvesting her memory of him in the communication of the good news of the resurrection of Christ, the Lord. At this moment, her witness continues to you and me.

But the most severe griefs are the loss of a spouse or a child. Holmes and Masuda, in their extensive research on stress, rank the death of a spouse as the most severe stress a person has to endure.[8] This may be true of hospitalized patients who formed the population of the study. Yet, outside a hospital and in a day-to-day parish situation, the death of a child vies for first place in devastation of a family. Hence, we shall pay equal attention to the death of a spouse and the death of a child.[9]

The Death of a Spouse

Many continuing emotions attend the death of a spouse, depending upon the depth of intimacy and length of years of the marriage. Velma Stevens, an author who has been twice widowed, in her book, *Grief Work*, lists the following emotions:

- Shock, disbelief, and numbness
- Sorrow
- Loss of meaning
- Anger, hostility and guilt
- Fear
- Loneliness
- Depression
- Acceptance, resignation, and peace

She does not suggest a time sequence of stages for these emotions. The emotions seem to be a collage of feelings that defy a neat order of appearance, although a process of working through them is evident.

For the last five years my wife and I have grieved alongside a colleague of mine whose wife died after a two-year battle with cancer involving the colon, the liver, three surgeries, and a siege of severe pain. He was twenty years older than she, inasmuch as his first wife died giving birth to their third child. His present wife's parents both had lived into their late nineties and never had cancer. She herself had no carcinogenic habits such as drinking or smoking. She lived a very rigorous life as an extremely successful public school teacher; she had a master's and doctorate in education. She preferred teaching middle school children.

His reactions were, first, great grief, and then rage at the injustice of her dying first, even though she was twenty years younger than he. He felt that the Almighty had done her and him an injustice. Anger is a legitimate response to injustice. He felt that he—who had survived two bypass surgeries—should have been the one to die.

Along with the rage, he was both grieved and comforted by distinct sensings of her presence, her remembered sayings and wisdom, and her tender love for him. Long after her death he receives letters, telephone calls, and visits from her former students for whom she had been a mentor. Some of them did not know of her death.

His long-term emotion is loneliness. This loneliness takes a characteristic form of *social displacement*. He is too often left out of social events because he has no one with him and does not feel free to go by reason of his being a single widower. For women who are widows such experiences can be intense. As Velma Stevens says, "Loss of status and self-worth comes with the death of a mate. It is painful to be labeled 'widow' or 'widower' after proudly bearing the title 'wife' or 'husband'. . . . Persons know how to be husbands or wives. No one knows how to be a widow or widower."[10]

My colleague and friend had through many years made lasting friendships. These have assuaged, not healed, the loneliness he has to bear. A pastor can himself or herself be enriched by regular times of reflection and mutual sharing with such a widow or widower. My wife's and my friendship with both this widower colleague has been more than a formal pastoral relationship; it has been a pilgrimage filled with meaning and spiritual enrichment. If a formal pastor can participate in the long-term care of lonely widowers and widows, care that obscures the boundaries of appropriateness at all times, both parties can experience great mutuality and edification in which everybody gains in a context of thoughtfulness and kindness.

Probably one of the classic records of the responses of a bereaved person at the death of a spouse is C. S. Lewis' *A Grief Observed*.[11] Cancer claimed his wife, Joy, after three years of a very happy marriage. Chad Walsh, who wrote an afterword to Lewis's autobiographical account, was a close friend of Lewis. He says that after Joy's death, he and Lewis "sensed we could share some portion of the deep agony that he experienced in his dark night of the soul."[12]

Lewis's own his loss of his wife was compounded by his earlier loss of his mother and father. He says: "Cancer, cancer cancer. My mother, my father, my wife. I wonder who is next in the queue." His wife, Joy, died on June 13, 1960. Chad Walsh says that Lewis never recovered from losing her. "He was subdued and at loose ends. His own health began to fail. He had a combination of heart and kidney ailments; the attempt to alleviate one condition would aggravate the other." [13] He died three years after Joy died, on November 22, 1963, the same day President Kennedy was assassinated.

I had twenty-two funerals in the first year of my pastorates. But rarely do we pastors realize the healing and learning grace of forming and maintaining long-term, reciprocal relationships with persons bereaved of a spouse. The kind of friendship Chad Walsh had with C. S. Lewis is exemplary of what a powerful conveyor of the presence of God this kind of pilgrimage can be. In the great emphases on megachurches today, as well as the extreme formalizations of pastoral counseling, the pastoral depths of a life-long pilgrimage with a bereaved person are lost. It is a costly discipleship, but is also an enriching and rewarding one.

Lewis wrote of his spiritual disputations with God in his grief. First he spoke of his wife:

> My love for her was of much the same quality as my faith in God. . . . Whether there was anything but imagination in the faith, or anything but egoism in the love, God knows, I don't. . . . But oh God, tenderly, tenderly. Already, month by month and week by week you broke her body on the wheel whilst she still wore it. Is it not yet enough?[14]

In his resolution of a long debate with God, often filled with anger, Lewis decides. He earlier was concerned that his memory of his wife might become false. "For some reason—the merciful good sense of God is the only one I am thinking of—I have stopped bothering about that . . . since I stopped bothering about it, she seems to meet me everywhere. *Meet* is far too strong a word. . . . Rather, a sort of unobtrusive but massive sense that she is, just as much as ever, a fact to be taken into account."[15]

Stevens and Lewis give us a very articulate and inspiring understanding of what grief is like in a healthy person. However, the darkest side of grief appeared on last night's local news. A wife had shot her husband to death. Other reports of men shooting their girlfriends or wives appear with a numbing frequency. Somebody has the task of conducting these funerals, too, and of comforting the parents and children, if any, of the murdered persons. Getting through the legal and penal systems to the perpetrators is another thing. We need research reports from prison chaplains as to what kind of grief the perpetrator of the murder of his or her spouse experiences. I bring this issue into our discussion because this pathological sort of death of a spouse at the violent hands of the other is a part of our daily news, but has not, to my knowledge been mentioned much less researched by pastors.

The Death of a Son or Daughter

The impact of the death of a child upon a family—parents and siblings—is well within the attention, research, and observation of pastors. The most recent death of a child that came to my attention was the stillbirth of the child of one of my colleagues and his wife. I spoke with the father, expressing my concern and devotion to him at this difficult time in his and his wife's life, particularly his wife. I spoke to him of the total frustration that she particularly might feel after having gone through a whole pregnancy cycle and then to have the child be dead at birth. He said that she moved in and out of depression. He spoke of their other three children and their grief. Yet, I said to him, no one can take this child's place.

Beverly Raphael again reports the experience of a twenty-year-old mother in conversation with her doctor after the birth of her child; "Then I said, 'I want to see my baby, doctor.' He said, 'No, you can't, Mrs. King—its no good, the baby's dead—it will only give you bad memories to take away. It would be better if you put it out of your mind.' Then he hurried away as though he were ashamed or something—maybe so he wouldn't see me cry."[16]

A physician with whom I worked was more secure in his wisdom about motherhood. He said, "No one is as paranoid as a mother who has not yet seen her newborn baby." The above-mentioned doctor left the mother with an empty set of feelings. Her suspicions about her baby's whereabouts will be filled with her interpretation of the doctor's withholding the truth or even telling her a falsehood. She had earned the right to *see* her baby—dead or alive. She could take that much more easily than not seeing her baby at all.

Spontaneous Miscarriage

Pastoral attention to the grief of parents who have lost a child by miscarriage is sparse. Pastors are too ready to convey conventional insensitivity: "That's too bad. I hope the mother is in good health." Or, "You can after a little while have another child." These and other such remarks overlook the frustration, loss, and continuing fear miscarriage creates. The mother may fear that she will never have another child and be plagued with fear and depression if she does become pregnant. If the couple's fertility has been in doubt, the miscarriage may be a double grief. Repetitive miscarriages influence one other and prompt despair. Pastoral care must include full recognition of this as a real grief situation. The populace tends to ignore the event to the extent that many couples keep this a secret, even when the miscarriage occurs in later pregnancy after baby's movements have been felt or even seen in the sonograph screen. As one mother said: "They said it was nothing. . . just a miscarriage. I was only a few weeks overdue. I had seen those pictures, and I knew it was only tiny, but it as *my baby*, and it counted as a real family."[18]

Abortion

A miscarriage is a spontaneous abortion. This occurs often, my medical advisors tell me, when there is not enough gene material in the fetus to sustain life. The purpose of this section is to discuss the grief and separation that follow the termination of a pregnancy by medically induced abortion. The larger political and ideological debate is important but regularly omits the discussion of the bereavement that ensues after an abortion. This event may be done under the best of medical conditions. Nevertheless, many women and in some cases fathers of the child suffer grief and shame. The event becomes a secret difficult to share because few listeners can be trusted with the information. This leaves the woman isolated in her grief. No community of grief gathers around her. One aspect of the unwanted pregnancy is the threat of suicide on the part of the pregnant mother. Having worked as a professor of psychiatry in a school of medicine for many years, I saw that in the case of an attempted suicide of a pregnant mother, a medically approved decision was necessary for an abortion even before it was legalized. A committee of physicians had to agree that the mother's life was at stake before this agreement became a decision of the panel of physicians. Suicide of the mother would end two lives and not just one.

Such extreme reactions on the part of a mother only occasionally occur in the present day. Nevertheless, "the pattern of grief and mourning is not dissimilar to that for spontaneous abortion, except that suppression and inhibition of grief are much more likely."[18] Add to this the coercion of the woman's parents for her to have a secret abortion or their rejecting her completely. It is little wonder that in addition to mourning her loss of her baby, she feels, as one said, "black and dirty inside."

A pastor who has the opportunity to minister to a woman usually does so after the fact of the abortion. This must be a privileged communication in which neither shares the information with anyone else without the other's permission. Whatever else a pastor may think or feel about abortion, the forgiveness and comfort of God in the Lord Jesus Christ must be communicated with our own compassion. Abortion is not the unpardonable sin. Unforgiveness is (see Matthew 6:14-15). A steadfast relationship of trust needs to be established. One reason for this is that repeated unplanned pregnancies and terminations may occur later. Substantive pastoral care may be a deterrent to these further tragedies.

The Birth of a Malformed Child

Hereditary malformations, gestational or congenital disorders, and birth defects may result in spontaneous abortions. As has been said, such events occur in about half the cases, my medical consultants tell me. Many pregnancies go on to full term. An anencephalic child is an example, that is, a child born without a brain. This is a congenital malformation in which none or very little of the brain forms in the development of the fetus. Such babies are often born to live only a short while.

The parents are bitterly fortunate when the child mercifully does not live long as a completely uncoordinated and unaware being. Yet, it is *their* child, and they suffer a double grief.

A pastor does well to offer a simple but profound funeral—probably including the parents, siblings, grandparents and other close relatives and friends. Thus the grief is taken out of secret and a grieving community is formed that surrounds the parents and siblings with support.

Many other malformations leave the child physically whole but severely disabled. Just to name a few—cerebral palsy, children born without one or more limbs, the many kinds of mental retardation, deafness, blindness, speechlessness—are examples. These are to the parents chronic sorrows. Nevertheless such disabled children can be a source of joy for their parents because holding, touching, hugging, kissing, and simply being with the child are nonverbal forms of communication between them and their child.

Two precautions: first, never leap to the conclusion that a disabled child is therefore mentally deficient. I have participated in the ordination of a woman with cerebral palsy who is an honors graduate of the University of Richmond, Union Theological Seminary in New York, and the New York School of Social Work. She served as a chaplain at the Long Island, New York, Institute for Cerebral Palsy. She is retired now but does consultant work. Her name is Virginia Kreyer, and we have remained in touch by mail since 1954. Second, do not assume that the parents of this child are perpetually unhappy. They are not. They have their beatific days, discovering unexpected gifts in their disabled son or daughter.

Richard Landon, pastor of the Trinity Baptist Church in Lexington, Kentucky, is a good role model for all pastors in the care of disabled persons, particularly mentally retarded ones. His pilgrimage began with having a retarded brother in his own family of origin. In his pastorate he saw to it that Sunday school classes were formed for retarded persons. Uniquely, he organized a class for *adult* retarded persons. They became members of the church as well. The class had well over fifty members! A repeated crisis occurred, however: the aging parents of these mentally disabled adults began to die. No one wanted their adult sons and daughters. Richard Landon, his official board, congregation and many businesses in the city, aided by television stations, raised money for a farm nearby called Quest Farm. This became a well staffed home and place of work, a simplified environment for retarded adults. The farm has built additional buildings and continues as a witness to what can be done, not just to comfort, but to care substantially for mentally disabled persons. These persons do not "fall through the cracks" of overloaded, overstressed underfunded state, county, and city welfare agencies that, nevertheless, need all the appreciation, encouragement and support we can provide them.

Murdered Children

When you and I listen to the local evening news, we do not have the option of assuming that death is far from children, young people, and adults by homicide in the homes and streets of our communities. We hear much of these deaths and opt out with apathy. It is much more demanding to become a part of comfort to these young people's parents. Putting thousands more police on the streets is, of course, some major help. At the root of many of these deaths, however, is the disintegration of neighborhoods. Even in the suburbs, a neighbor can die, be buried, and a next-door neighbor never know. Our neighbors need not be next door. They may live across the city and stay in touch by phone. But many people do not do so. They become social isolates, recluses. Inner city neighborhoods have suffered more. With the desegregation of schools, the neighborhood school, inferior though it was, ceased to be a neighborhood institution. A parent of a child in our east end cannot easily participate in a parents' organization in a school in central city nor can a parent in our west end attend parents' organizations in the east end.

Since the 1960s, more aggressive and motivated African Americans have entered the middle classes and moved out of the ghettoes. Inspiring role models for children remain few. The upsurge of the single parent home—both Caucasian and African American—has encouraged many fathers into irresponsibility for their children. Grammar school and high school boys find their support, role models, and pattern of action in street gangs. The gang's authority replaces that of the father. Hence, drugs, murder, and mayhem become substitutes for jobs in a highly unemployed population of school dropouts.

The African-American church has stayed put in the neighborhoods. The pastors are becoming increasingly involved as community leaders. Through the organizations of our churches Caucasian pastors in the suburbs can form liaisons of comfort, support, and consolation to bereaved parents—usually mothers—of murdered children. The very least a pastor can do is to write letters to each mother and father, telephone them, attend or conduct funerals, and gather funds for the family to pay for a funeral. This is not a one-way street of care. The pastor is rewarded with friends he or she would never otherwise have met. Life will become more meaningful and less parochial in the ministry of pastor and congregation.

Murder and murder-suicides are not restricted to ghetto areas. They are occurring in the suburbs, too. Pastoral attention to these situations is a form of spreading the good news of the presence of the living Christ. A pastor cannot do all this by himself or herself; to the contrary, church members who live near or are intimate friends of the victims can respond as well.

LOSSES IN LATER MATURITY

Separation and grief blend in the lives of persons above the age of sixty-five. We already have been through such transitions as the children's leaving home, their divorces (if they shall have happened), the dispersing of many of our friendship groups. Now we face retirement years without the support group of our fellow workers. These latter relationships are maintained—if at all—by letters, telephone calls, and occasional visits when they return to our location or we go to see them.

Grandchildren, Sons, and Daughters

Grandchildren, if there are any, may provide great satisfaction or represent a constant worry if they drop out of school, get into trouble with the law, join the drug population, and so on. If, however, they are high achievers in school, athletics, or work, and if they have an affectionate preference for and bond with us, they are a sustaining grace to us.

Our concern about grandchildren is the extension of our history with our sons and our daughters. The desire for our own perpetuity after we are gone is closely allied with our pleasure or displeasure with the way our sons and daughters "turn out." The departure of sons or daughters from "the ways we reared them" is a separation in itself. The subtle rippage of grown sons and daughters from their parents' social class through upward and downward mobility takes its human toll on aging parents' dreams for their offspring.

Thus, one of the least spoken bereavements of older people is "the death of a dream" for their nuclear family. When a daughter or son contracts and dies with AIDS or is imprisoned for a felony, a speechless grief is mollified at the most by close friends in whom parents can confide. The pastoral care of the families and church communities of AIDS patients is clinically described in William Amos's book, *When AIDS Comes to Church* [19]. But I am not aware of the pastors' and churches' response to the parents, grandparents, and children of people in prison. If the community of prison chaplains has such information, I heartily ask of them that they share it with all of us in some written form. Letters are a great source.

The Death of Friends

It has been said that people know they are getting old when the obituaries are the first section of the paper they read! They are looking for the names of people to whom they have been close at one time or another in their lives. Many times these names are those they recently or presently care for as long-term friends or relatives. They find themselves attending fewer weddings and more funerals. A pastor ministers to them in funeral groups. Another way of doing so is to help arrange a memorial service in which friends can also express memories and appreciation of the deceased. A follow-up visit, telephone call, or letter is a further ministry. Most helpful are serendipitous conversations when you meet in the grocery, at the post office, after a public school function, or simply tarry after a service at the church.

At this time, from my study at home and in Louisville, Kentucky, I am in touch with a life-long friend's widow in San Francisco, two aged friends in North Carolina, one of whom is in a retirement home and the other in a nursing home, and the spouse of a dying husband in Missouri. "Staying connected" with them is not just a pastoral ministry to them; it is a renewing grace to me to be in touch with them while possible.

Bodily Losses

Grief is a much more intrapersonal reality for aged persons than for younger people, although these particular losses are often the lot of young and younger persons as well.

• *Loss of Work.* Retirement from work often removes the core of meaning for aging persons. This is particularly true of persons who have only one means of earning money. The financial jolt is a depressing loss. Persons who can turn a hobby into a second career are very fortunate. Many people who can afford it and are physically able replace work with travel. More subtle in the loss of work is the loss of daily contact with meaningful coworkers.

• *Loss of Hearing.* Not to be able to hear narrows our communication with people, especially where public speeches are being made. I myself am deaf in my right ear. My audiologist fitted a transmitter for my right ear and a receiver for my good ear. The transmitter sends sounds from my right ear to the receiver in my left ear!

We have a new pastor who will preach his first sermon on this coming Sunday. He invited four of us older persons, who let him know we could not hear well, to the sanctuary, where he and the sound crew tested out the acoustics of the building and effectiveness of the public address system. He made it an inspiring occasion by giving us a recitation of large sections of the Sermon on the Mount. In the process, no mention was made of any conspicuous devices for the hearing impaired. We were considered like any other segment of the congregation.

• *Loss of Sight.* This loss involves a larger loss—of easy mobility. One can no longer drive a car. This loss begins early, at about forty. Loss of sight is gradual and is deferred by the use of glasses, medical and surgical treatment for glaucoma and cataracts. The obstinacy of many people against using glasses and hearing aids (with good batteries) makes these impediments all the more difficult.

• *Loss of Sexual Function.* Kinsey was one of the first to examine the effects of age on sexual function. (Recall that "David was old and advanced in years . . . so they searched for a beautiful girl throughout all the territory of Israel and found Abishag the Shunammite and brought her to the king, . . . but the king did not know her sexually" [1 Kings 1:1-4].)

Impotence is more of a trauma for men than women, as if a very important part of their person has died. It progresses: erection takes longer, then the penis becomes more flaccid, and the amount of semen is reduced with less need to ejaculate, until the time that no sexual function is possible.[20]

A minority of aging persons maintain a stable and somewhat active sexual pattern into the eighties and nineties. But loss of this ability is attended by shock and sadness. It has to be borne in secrecy by many modern people. This loss need not destroy sexual tenderness of hugging, kissing, fondling, and holding. Laughter and expressions of affection can with imagination continue the vividness of sexuality. If a couple have learned the skill and devotion to put loving and sexual feelings into words, they can express sexuality the way they did in their courtship before they ever had sexual intercourse. Coitus is not the only way to be sexual. God's creation of sensual pleasure can continue throughout a couple's lifetime.

• *The Loss of Bodily Functions.* The inability to urinate and/or defecate are life threatening losses of bodily functions. The impairment of the ability to walk unaided by another person, a cane, crutch, wheelchair, or electrical runabout makes a person heavily dependent. Strokes, fluctuating blood pressure, accidents such as a broken hip, and advanced cases of diabetes are a few of the causes of disability in the loss of bodily functions.

• *The Loss of Mental Awareness.* Severe brain changes can remove a people's awareness and orientation. They lose orientation as to where they are, when it is, and—worse—who they are and who even their closest friends and relatives are. For their relatives this loss presents a profound grief coupled with a major stress in caring for them. More often now these patients are diagnosed with Alzheimer's disease, although careful neurological and psychiatric attention should agree upon this diagnosis. Sometimes it is a functional expression of a stuporous depression, a treatable disorder.

Churches can organize Alzheimer's day care centers to socialize the patients in a Christian community and to give the regular, over stressed caretakers a respite. Alzheimer's patients, like little children, can respond to kinds of blessing, arms of affection, and preferred foods. However, they can in the latter stages become belligerent and seek to hurt those who are helping them. For example, one man sought to hit his wife with a chair. Fortunately, she slipped out and locked a back door before he could hit her. This incident became the signal that he needed to be in a skilled nursing home.

These many losses are more common in the aging process. A person of most ages, however, can suffer such losses through disease and accidents—especially industrial and auto accidents. A pastor can become informed about the medical nature of the disabilities by cumulative observations of many patients, collaboration with friendly physicians, and through owning a copy of *Merck's Manual of Diagnosis and Therapy.*[21] This can be bought inexpensively at a multipurpose bookstore. It provides background information in succinct form that enables a pastor to add discernment to the comfort offered patients and their families. Not the least of this discernment is the capacity to appreciate the course the illness takes. It helps to prepare for the shape of things to come both for the patient and his or her family. A part of pastoral ministry to aging persons is to be prepared to lower surprise, shock, and despair that occur when a new stage of the increasing loss happens. Surprise, shock, and despair are component emotions of panic which throw the whole system into alarm. A pastor can, with comfort, reassurance, and knowledge, forestall and prevent panic, which only makes bad matters worse. Panic is a part of the grief process at losing vital bodily functions.

SUICIDE

In this discussion of grief and separation in the life cycle, only a little has been said about the pastoral care of families surviving a person who has completed a suicide. Suicide occurs at most of the phases of the life cycle. Transitions from one period of the life cycle to another are times when suicide is contemplated. For example, a twenty-three-year-old man who finished college in May came to see me this week. This is September and he has not yet found a job. He is still dependent on his parents. He has little idea as to what he can do with his education. He is depressed and speaks of suicide.

Furthermore, depression often sets in at retirement, accompanied by suicidal thoughts. A pastor who pays attention to these transitions, develops church rituals for recognizing them, and enables the congregation to provide encouragement and assistance at these crisis transitions will go far toward preventing suicide. For example, a job-search program within the congregation for people of all ages can be spiritual service.

Even so, suicides occur. One schizophrenic mother, divorced, with a ten-year-old son was terror-stricken that someone was plotting to steal her son. One night she took her father's shotgun and killed her sleeping son and herself. In another case, a depressed woman who had just been told by her husband that he was divorcing her, killed herself with carbon monoxide fumes from her garaged car. She had been threatening suicide for seventeen years, according to her husband. A middle-aged physician was a manic depressive. During the summer he was on a manic flight of activity. In January and February, he fell into a severe depression. During the first winter period, a group of us pulled him through. The manic flight in the summer distracted us. In the next February he took a shotgun one Wednesday at 4:00 a.m. and blew his head off. His files revealed a two-year series of suicide notes, the last of which said that he knew he was mentally ill, that there were medications for it, but he chose not to be a "zombie" on medication the rest of his life. He was a faithful member of his church. All my efforts to get him into treatment for a most treatable disorder had failed.

All these people had surviving families. Grief ministry to them is a pastor's challenge. Through the influence of the surviving leader of the family, the spouse, a grandparent, an aunt or uncle, the family as a whole can be gathered for planning of the funeral or memorial service. The questions, the guilt, the affirmations of the family can be explored as decisions about the funeral or memorial services are made.

After the crowd has thinned out, the more immediate family can be gathered for another debriefing and briefing session. It seems to me that suicide may be a ritual suicide at the loss of honor, such as the Japanese *hari kari* suicide and that of Saul (1 Sam. 28:31) or a *kamikaze* suicide such as the suicide bombers of Japan toward the close of World War II, or the Mideast car bombers of more recent years, and the suicide of Samson (Judg. 16:23–30). Or the suicide may be an acute expression of a mental illness that goes untreated. A pastoral example of a *hari kari* suicide is the implicated person in a criminal trial who kills himself or herself before going to trial, taking any evidence along. The church member who kills himself rather than have the church split asunder by conflict over him seems to be akin to the kamikaze death. These latter two kinds of suicide are far outnumbered by the acutely mentally ill persons in the church. The families can have a few of their questions answered by the information above.

Individuals in the family or the family as a whole may want reading material. John Hewett's book *After Suicide*[22] is an excellent resource. For the pastor's own use, my book, *Pastor's Handbook*[23] deals with "the Pastoral Care of Families in the Aftermath of Suicide."

Longer term issues in the continuing care of the survivors of suicide that require pastoral awareness and attention are:

1. The pain of the family members at not being consulted about the planned suicide or the impulsive suicide. Not all suicides are planned, but practically all are completed in secrecy, and the family member is left out and has no chance to help or to say good bye.

2. The superstition that all persons who commit suicide go to hell. This grows out of a belief that suicide is a sin. According to this belief,

the person has no chance for asking forgiveness or to express repentance; therefore, he or she goes to hell alienated from God. Yet, this belief limits the power and wisdom of God to search the heart of a suicidal person. Unto God all hearts are open and from God no secrets are hid.

3. The life-long tendency of families to hold this as a secret. Frederick Buechner makes this the centerpiece of his book on *Secrets* in which he tells of the death of his father. Inasmuch as my own father committed suicide, I kept this fact a secret for a long time. But, as I grew past college, I had formed close, long-term, mature friendships with colleagues with whom I did not need to hold this secret. In older years, one of the gifts is not to worry about secrets that involve no one but yourself!

A further source of fellowship and guidance is provided by many comprehensive mental health centers for families surviving suicide. A pastor of the person traumatized can ask for the SOS group schedule and location—Survivors of Suicide. These groups are open to and for the public and are for sharing of suffering, instruction, and inspiration by trained leaders, some of whom are clergy.

4

GRIEF AND SEPARATION
IN DIVORCE

Elie Wiesel says: "I am in favor of welcoming as many foreigners as generously as possible. Whoever needs a refuge must feel welcome wherever I am. If he (or she) is a foreigner in my country, then I will be one, too."[1]

Wiesel was not talking about marriage and divorce but, whether we believe it or not, the kinds of acquaintances that get Americans married still leaves them as foreigners or strangers to each other and to themselves in relation to each other. Conditions of alienation and abandonment that are implicit, nonverbal, and unconscious to each partner lie like deep waters in the depths of each marital partner. Unadmitted and even unknown assumptions abound in each person's mind. These assumptions can—and, as they surface, often do—unattended and uncorrected, become the divisive forces that lead to alienation, grief, and separation.

Divorce is one of the most wrenching of these alienations, separations, and griefs. Two people marry as acquaintances, at best, or as strangers and foreigners to each other, at worst. Part of this is because of the fragmented nature of our society. We are no longer a close-knit community where men and women grow up together, know each other's families of origin, and know each other from childhood. We are in our own ways foreigners to each other in terms of the intimacies marriage entails.

More profound, however, are the nonverbal and unconscious assumptions that women and men both privately and unconsciously expect of one another before marriage. In these nonverbal and unconscious arenas, they are indeed foreigners and strangers. As these become expressed to one another and semiconscious within each individual, conflict and alienation become more manifest. The marriage gets into trouble—real trouble.

Clifford Sager, M.D., and his several colleagues have said that the marriage contract—or, as I would put it, covenant—can be made at the conscious, verbal level; the conscious but not verbalized level; and the level beyond awareness.[2]

At the conscious, verbal level, a particular couple Sager cites—the man, 34, and the woman, 24—agreed that men and women are equal and able to take care of themselves without being helplessly dependent. They could help each other in different ways. He could be useful in her advancement professionally. She could help him sexually because he was "sexually inadequate and inexperienced and vulnerable."

At the conscious but not verbalized level, she felt anxious and afraid professionally. She was jealous of his professional competence. They were in competition both at work and in bed. He wanted her to go into another field professionally so that they would not be in competition. On the other side, he privately wanted "many women," and he expected her to empower him sexually so he would be adequate. "I expect you to do this for everything I do for you."

At the unconscious level, she wanted his power as a male to "control, dominate, and compete." She would not abandon him if he would let her destroy his dominance. She both wanted him to have other women, and yet he must do this for her. If he did not, she would make him sexually free. She wanted them to be *both* close and intimate *and* distant and separate. He in turn continued to want other women with her permission and protection. He thought he would make her powerful to dominate him in return. Yet, at the same time, he felt that women were inferior; he intended to dominate her, and if she capitulated to this, he would not hurt or abandon her. Little wonder that this woman was anxious and depressed, and he was insecure sexually and made up for it on his job as a teacher in a school in which she was a student.[3]

When the conscious, nonverbal, and unconscious realities erupted, these two strangers were attempting the impossible. The marriage was at serious risk for divorce with all its conflict, disillusionment, alienation, and grief. The conditions of alienation and abandonment were inherent in the relationship from the outset. At least the conscious, unspoken convictions could have been shared if enough trust and freedom from the fear of rejection were not keeping these secrets from the other partner.

Yet, when the unconscious, unaware contradictions come to the surface and the marriage is at risk for divorce, then rage and guilt, fear and brutality of abuse make the grief and separation excruciatingly painful. Kevin T. Keely rightly says, "Marriage breakdown is a form of dying. . . . Especially for the partners in the marriage there is a crushing sense of rejection and personal failure."[4] Consequently, this chapter is devoted to assessing this kind of grief and separation and the pastoral care of the victims.

I say "victims" advisedly, because everyone related to the divorce—children, grandparents, friends—add their sorrow to that of the divorcing couple. A variety of events occurs in the movement of a couple toward divorce. They do not necessarily follow a pattern. The reason is that the couple will have a variety of efforts at reconciliation. Thus they have several starts toward divorce that are reversed by attempts to reconcile them by family members, friends, and counselors. In addition they themselves initiate efforts to get back together. Some families go through years of threatening divorce. One family alternated for seventeen years between the husband's threats of divorce and the wife's threats of suicide if he divorced her. It culminated in her killing herself one morning with carbon monoxide from car fumes in their enclosed garage. In this way did "death part" them.

With these qualifying reservations about progression toward divorce, let us consider the following ingredients that people must keep in mind as they move toward a divorce.

THE COURSE OF DIVORCE

Every couple goes through adjustmental conflicts, usually in the first year or two of marriage. However, these conflicts can become chronic. Couples that have been married for thirty years have been found fighting over these concerns. Here are some stages in marital conflict.

1. An agreed-upon schedule of times and responsibilities that meets both partners' needs is important. Work schedule, eating and sleeping

routines, household chores, recreational events, and church going are a few of the adjustments to be agreed upon. Agreement on friendships with people outside the couple's private relationship as well as meeting expectations of in-laws are a part of early adjustments. Conflict in this area usually takes the form of irritable snappings at each other over minute things, pouting and refusing to speak, periodic blasts of rage, and depression. Underneath all of this there may be sexual difficulties in performance or overdemanding behavior to compensate for the general malaise of the relationship.

Whereas a large number of couples go through these adjustmental conflicts with humor, readiness to accept responsibility for errors, forgiveness, and a growth of intimacy, for the divorce-prone the depression and irritability are the first signs of grief and separation. One major preventive approach by pastors is to lead a group of newlyweds who come to his or her church. They can invite friends of theirs who are newly wed but have no church affiliation. Biblical wisdom could be an "opener" for discussion, such as 1 Peter 3:7. Specific issues of early adjustment such as those mentioned above can provide a "curriculum" for further discussions. The group itself can form its own agenda. An important result of such a group, if led by the pastor, is that the pastor forms a lasting relationship to couples as a couple, and he makes himself available when more serious conflicts arise.

2. Gradual withdrawal of the couple from each other and the development of parallel lives may occur. Here the couple quietly give up trying to adjust to each other. They are coolly civil with each other, deal with such things as meal preparation, laundry, keeping the bills paid, and meeting outsiders with a kind of display of concern for each other that covers anything wrong. They may seem to other people as the "perfect couple." Underneath this, however, is a quiet desperation and lives lived parallel to each other, each going her or his way, neither moving toward or away from each other in intimacy, on the one hand, or hostility, on the other hand. In the words of a popular song of a few years ago: "These are the days of dancing six feet apart."

Pastoral outreach toward such a couple with this behavior is very difficult. The last person they want to touch their bruised spirits is the pastor. They are afraid he will tell their parents or become *too* concerned.

After all, no real mention of divorce has yet appeared. A house call, the ultimate in pastoral initiative, may reveal the story. If the pastor has a prior relationship of having done premarital counseling, and if he or she has a standard ritual of home visits to bless the new home and to pray there for the couple, then he or she is well situated for a more intimate query: "All couples have the temptation for each to go his or her own way as if he or she has a roommate and not a marriage partner. How has this temptation served you?" This is a surgical question and yet it may be a well-placed lancing of infection.

Another approach is even more emphatic. Marriage multiplies rather than divides in half the number of things that stress a person. How about the stresses of making a living, keeping finances straight, tending to the expectations of in-laws, and such? "How are the new stresses normal to marriage treating you?"—this is a good question to ask. Courtship is built around play; marriage is built around work. First marriages tend to happen in much the same time-frame as do efforts to get securely established on a job. The combined stresses flow into each other and it becomes difficult to tell one from the other. Fatigue is a real enemy of intimacy.

These are all a part of adjustmental conflicts. Other conflicts can arise. The young and not-so-young married couple, as in the case reported above, may be in a silent power struggle about who is going to dominate whom. Female equality is a part of this. Some men may give lip service to female equality while they nonverbally and unconsciously carry the heavy imprint of their parents' way of life—that women are inferior to men.

Getting this issue out on the table and talking about it, each learning from the other, develops a working covenant that is open and honest. If this conversation does not happen, the issue becomes chronic and puts more distance between them. Such issues can be a vital part of group discussion led by a pastor for newlyweds.

This stage of parallel lives is the time a couple best deals with the unspoken, nonverbal but conscious issues of their relationship. False and unworkable assumptions can be laid upon the table in marital counseling. A pastoral counselor or a marriage and family therapist can be of real help to a couple who still have an intact marriage and want to enrich and secure their understanding of each other.

3. Serious breaches of the covenant and the emergence of a "private misunderstanding" may occur. Grief and separation happen at the serious breaches of the covenant between a couple. Major deceptions emerge, such as in the case of the man who had not told his wife that he had a prison record for having committed a felony. The truth emerged when they sought to buy a house and his prison record was found in the background check as a part of making a loan. Remarkably enough, they talked through the issue and she forgave his deception. The marriage remained intact, but the purchase of a house had to be in her name only, and she was solely responsible for payment.

More serious deceptions are involved when a member of the couple learns that his or her spouse has children by another person. Most damaging is the revelation that one or the other has an affair going at the time. Often this is what brings a couple into counseling. The person having the affair is tempted to continue it. This may be so even if the pastoral counselor gets an agreement that the unfaithful partner will cease and desist from the affair. The "offended" partner may have a compulsion to play detective, checking the every move of the spouse. More affluent spouses may employ a private detective to do this.

This subterfuge on both their parts sabotages an honest attempt at healing the breach and trying to discover some of the contributing causes of the infidelity.

Another serious breach of the covenant is the attempt by relatives of either or both spouses to control the relationship of the couple. One or the other spouse's parents actually or allegedly reject the spouse not related to them. For example, the father of a man whose wife found him in the acts of an affair intervened and forced a remarriage after a divorce by, in effect, bribing the wife to return to the marriage with his son. The whole counseling process was destroyed by the father of the son, and father-in-law of the wife! Things have difficulty getting worse than this!

Pastoral intervention at the stage of a private misunderstanding is very unlikely. The couple have an almost unwritten code not to share their desperation with anyone. A pastor may *sense* the desperation by noticing the separate attendance of the couple or noticing their depressed features or hyperactive busyness with which they ward off their grief and separation.

4. The events of social involvement occur. The isolation of the couple is broken when they separately or together decide to share their plight of grief and separation with other people. The optimum pastoral situation is when they turn separately or together to the counselor first. Thus, he or she can discuss with them with whom they will talk next. This same advantage is that of the formal pastoral counselor to whom they may turn with the request that he not share the facts with others. Such an agreement needs to be mutual. The couple should agree not to share this with others without first conferring with the pastor and/or the pastoral counselor. Otherwise he or she may be accused of spreading the news around the community. What happens is the couple tells others who in turn tell even others. Then the husband and/or wife have other people to ask them about their situation. They assume that the pastor has broken his or her "confidentiality." Hence, it is far better to have a covenant of privileged communication than to promise confidentiality. Privileged communication means that each will confer with the other before telling the information to a third party.

This is the *orderly* way of managing the information when the pastor is the first confidante. Rarely does it happen this way. Too often a third partner, a paramour, another man or woman is told that things are in bad shape between husband and wife. Sooner or later the other partner becomes suspicious, watches the telephone calls made or received, checks for smudged lipstick on shirts, follows the spouse and catches him or her with the other man or woman. Then the shattered covenant is further compromised by an affair, more bluntly described as adultery.

Even in marital therapy the counseling relationship can be brought to a sudden halt when the offended spouse learns that, in spite of the promise to stop it during therapy, the affair continues. The difficulty of "turning off" an affair far outdistances the ease with which it was "turned on." The offending party is faced with the great difficulty of ending a relationship when their other lover will have no such thing. They refuse to be turned off. They "diesel."

Relatives of the couple—parents, siblings, uncles, aunts, grandparents—are often told of the difficulty the marriage is in. Often these persons are mature and wise enough to be a catalyst for reconciliation. If this does not happen, the relatives turn supportive of their own kin or pronounce a curse on both partners. In the latter instance, they increase the isolation of the couple. Friends outside the family are often more helpful than kin folks because they can maintain more objectivity.

62   GRIEF, TRANSITION, AND LOSS

The persons outside the family often consulted too soon are lawyers. Secretly, each partner consults his or her lawyer. By the time the couple come to the attention of the pastor or pastoral counselor, the couple may already be in the process of litigation. A pastor can do some preventive preaching and teaching by interpreting 1 Cor. 6:1-7, which urges that the fellowship of the Christian community, instead of the legal authorities of the secular world, should be sought regarding misunderstandings in "matters pertaining to this life." Such teaching and preaching is best done when no particular situation is fretting the families in the church.

Nevertheless, couples prematurely seek the services of lawyers, a few of whom are primarily concerned with arbitration and reconciliation of the marriage. This group's numbers are growing in their commitment to mediation vs. adversarial work with couples. The most disastrous legal event that can occur is when one partner goes to a lawyer first and then the other partner accompanies the first to the same lawyer. Then the lawyer is the advocate of the first and the adversary of the second partner. In my opinion, this behavior on the lawyer's part is deceptive and manipulative.

5. Separation. Some couples resort to separation before they get into the legal phase of divorce. Several kinds of separation are used. First, intramural separation happens when the couple cease to sleep, eat, have sex, or converse together. Yet, they stay in the same house and save rent by living intramurally, separated within the same walls. Second, the socially acceptable separation is often used. A couple may live in a large city, let us say. One spouse whose family lives in a small town or open country "goes home with the children" for the summer. Or, the husband has a job that requires that he travel more than usual. Or one of the partners decides to go on active duty in the military. These are ways of keeping the family finances in good shape and still be separated. Third, chaotic separation takes place when conflict reaches the level of verbal or physical abuse. One partner leaves the house for another shelter in order to be safe. Usually it is the woman who flees. We hear increasing numbers of reports in the media in which one or the other spouse kills the other in the face of an impending or completed divorce. Sometimes the killer then commits suicide. This marriage becomes a deadly game ending in divorce, murder, or suicide, or all three. The less violent chaotic separation comes when one partner leaves

when the rest of the family is absent. He or she, usually he, leaves a note saying that the marriage is over and he or she is leaving in this way so there will not be a big scene!

   6. The legal phase of divorce continues the grief and separation. If a couple have no children, very little money, and have been married only a short time, the conflict and sorrow can be very intense but are short-lived. It is easy enough for the couple to go their separate ways and never have anything to do with each other again. They may move long distances from each other and never see or hear of each other again.

   But, if they have children and even a modest set of financial assets, the grief work continues in legal battles over the custody of the children, the financial support of the children, the division of property, and the financial support of the mother of the children. Over these issues a running battle may ensue for four or five years or even longer.

   Even without these battles the grief continues at holiday times, at the weddings, hospitalizations, or funerals of children. The illusion that besets many people at the outset of divorce is that once they are divorced, it will be as if their partner will cease to exist. Their world will be as if he or she never existed. They are in for a rude awakening when the "other" partner keeps coming back into their lives like a day-waking nightmare.

   7. Post-divorce bereavement. Grief and separation in a divorce are different in kind from grief after death. In grief after death negative thoughts about the deceased get selectively unattended or even repressed. The time the deceased mate was unfaithful, wasted large sums of money, or even physically abused the mourner may be covered over in the mind of the bereaved person. The deceased is put on a pedestal and becomes an icon for the bereaved. The person may have been cremated and his or her ashes placed in a prominent place in the home.

   In divorce, just the opposite occurs. Only the negative, hateful, and derogatory things can be remembered. The positive, constructive and happy things are repressed, left unattended, and ignored. Rage takes the place of making an icon of the person. Nevertheless, the divorced spouse can become an icon of an evil sort. He or she can dominate the awareness of the bereaved in either a positive or negative way.

   Until bereaved persons can let go of these negative ruminations, they are not free to get on with the rest of their lives. They create problems for sons and daughters even when these are grown and never learn what the strengths and virtues of their divorced parents were. If sons or daughters do not join in the demonization of their divorced parent, they must go to other people who knew that parent for a more realistic view of the parent.

In some divorces—especially those without children and without large financial assets—the mourning in the grief and separation is acute, but it lasts a year or less. These marriages tend to be of brief duration—from one to three years. The seeds of destruction were germinating before or shortly after the wedding. The legal wrangling provides the forum for the suffering. Couples like this whom I have observed over a period of time seem to be reluctant to marry again. The phenomenon of living together without marriage seems to be an often chosen way of life. From a pastoral perspective, the corporate life of the church does not discuss "living together," although many senior citizens in the church have sons and daughters who are living together without marriage.

The grief and separation of divorce in families who have sons and daughters and considerable financial and real estate holdings tends to be chronic and sporadic. Sometimes the financial settlement stays in legal process for three or four years. The custody of minor children is an issue that is taken back to the court again and again. The anger, the disillusionment, and the sorrow extend over a long period of time.

One spiritual exercise tends to be absent from divorcing families: repentance and forgiveness. To see one's own wrong-doing and to repent, and ask forgiveness does not appear in case notes very often. The question is raised, "Is divorce a sin?" It is sin in the same way that living a deceptive, dishonest marriage is a sin, it seems to me. It is certainly not the unpardonable sin if the couple can find a realistic forgiveness for each other. Finding this goes a long way toward resolving the grief over the divorce.

DIVORCE: A METAPHOR FOR
HUMAN RELATIONSHIP OF ALL KINDS

Many relationships go through grief and separation although they have no legal binders such as do marriage relationships. The same alienation and abandonment plague these relationships. A few illustrative cases make this clear.

The bitterest of estrangement sometimes occurs when the property of a deceased person is being distributed to heirs. Legal contesting of a will can cause family infighting that can go unsettled for years. Even then relatives are estranged from each other in much the same kind of grief as divorce. If both parents die suddenly, as in a car or plane accident, battles over the custody of young children can become viciously controversial. Calm reasoning with professional help to assess the best interests of the children is not sought. To the contrary, the matter is taken to court. Long delays of legal procedures make the child or children all the more vulnerable.

Another example of grief similar to that of divorce can happen in the split up of business partners, or between employees and employers. As I write this, the whole baseball "industry" has come to a screeching halt because players and owners cannot agree. The damage to some individual families will be traumatic enough to equate it with the grief and sense of loss that divorced persons feel.

Partners in business who have worked harmoniously together for years can come to an impasse. One vulnerable spot in time is when sons or daughters, now grown, want to join the business. The other partner is adamantly opposed to the son or daughter coming aboard. Conflict arises and a breakup of the company is dynamically similar to that of divorce, even including at times extensive legal proceedings.

We as pastors become aware of such conditions of alienation, even among church members. For example, a colleague of mine was pastor of a county seat town in which most of the families were farmers. The church decided to build a new building. The vote to do so was unanimous except for one influential man in the church. He voted against it and was not asked for a reason. Later the pastor, who had a very good relationship with this man, asked him privately why he voted against the plan. The man readily said: "Well, for years a large family in the church has been feuding with me. I knew that if I voted for it, they would all vote against it. I voted against it and all of them voted for it." He was as wise as a serpent and as harmless as a dove! Such a story shows how these alienations affect the ways the church functions. A pastor becomes aware of them in unusual ways. A pastor works as a minister of reconciliation, not as an adversarial proponent of one side or the other.

An exact example of this is Jesus' response to the man who said, "'Teacher, tell my brother to divide the family inheritance with me.'

But he said to him, 'Friend, who set me to be a judge and arbitrator over you?'" (Luke 12:14). Jesus continues with the story of the man whose greed prompted him to build bigger barns and to say to his soul, "Soul, you have ample goods laid up for many years, relax, eat, drink and be merry." God spoke to him and said that that very night his life would be required of him. The goods he had acquired would be his relatives' to fight over the inheritance (Luke 12:15-21). In these fights, however, Jesus refused to be a judge and arbitrator. He instead pointed to the power of greed, the shortness of life, and to the importance of being "rich toward God" instead.

MARITAL INFIDELITY AND FIDELITY TO GOD

The book of Hosea takes marital relationship as a metaphor of our individual and corporate relationship to God. Hosea takes a prostitute, Gomer, as his wife who bore three children. Hosea's and Gomer's experience parallels that of Israel and God. Israel had been unfaithful to God, as Gomer was to Hosea. Hosea made strenuous efforts to renew the marriage and to begin all over again. He would "allure" her and "speak tenderly to her" and "give her vineyards." He would make a new covenant with her. "I will take you for my wife forever; I will take you for my wife in righteousness and in justice, in steadfast love, and in mercy. I will take you for my wife in faithfulness, and you shall know the Lord" (Hos. 2:14-20).

This spirit of reconciliation and forgiveness is at issue in Israel's relationship to God after Israel's having gone off in idolatry to worship Baal. In spite of Israel's ingratitude and infidelity to God, God would have compassion upon Israel: "It was I who taught Ephraim to walk, I took them up in my arms; but they did not know I healed them. I led them with cords of human kindness, with bands of love. I was to them like those who lift infants to their sleep, I bent down to them and led them" (Hos. 11:3-4).

In spite of this they kept sacrificing to Baals and offering incense to idols. For this God would punish them, but God also kept appealing to them for repentance and offers to "heal their disloyalty, and to love them freely and turn his anger from them" (Hosea 14:4). The similitude of our marital relationships to our relationship to God makes it a holy endeavor to be cared for with reverence for each other and the constant clarification and purification of our commitment to each other. Steadfast love and reverence for our covenant become acts of worship of God, forgiving each other with ready reconciliation with and reverence for each other.

5

WORK-RELATED GRIEF
AND SEPARATION

For the productive adult, a major portion of the day is spent in the workplace. Important personal relationships are formed there. If the workers serve in the same place over many years, these people-to-people relationships become deeply important, some of them quite positive and satisfying, and some of them quite negative and frustrating.

In addition to personal relationships, the workers have a distinct relationship to the company or institution as a whole and to its managerial staff, particularly the CEO, president, or executive secretary. This relationship can be a very dependent one. The individual worker becomes "emotionally and financially addicted to the good salaries, well appointed offices, and corporate benefits program. When people [are] fired or laid off in an era of extensive and irreversible cutbacks . . . that entitlement based world is collapsing and many . . . are finding it difficult to cut the cord."[1]

Though Carolyn Corbin enumerates only cutbacks, many other things are happening in the work world to produce the same results she mentions. In addition to the downsizing, for example, leveraged buyouts, mergers, and hostile takeovers are happening in increasing numbers.

In all these events, as well as individual firings, the worker goes through a severe experience of grief and separation. This chapter is devoted to an understanding on the part of pastors of this particular kind of separation and some pastoral approaches to caring for unemployed workers. This is very relevant to the work of a pastor whose church is like the churches in my hometown, Kannapolis, North Carolina. The Cannon Towel Company formerly *owned* the whole town! Under new management, this company is the dominant employer in the whole area. A pastor cannot avoid being affected by the actions of such a company. For example, a few years ago this company was sold by the Charles Cannon family to another owner, and massive changes took place. Under the Cannons' regime "mill houses" were rented to employees. Now those houses have been or are being sold to employees or, I assume, to anyone who can pay the price for them. Thus, one important dependency on the part of employees has been replaced by independence. Cannon's patriarchal grip on dependent employees was changed.

A case in point of paternalism is that of a candy manufacturer. He had a sense that *he* had to care for his employees. He worked as the CEO until he was eighty-five with the expressed concern that his employees—about five hundred of them—counted on him for a job. He gave them full benefits—medical insurance, retirement pay, sick leave, and vacations. His employees were predominantly skilled workers.

The other side of his expectations were that his employees had to be *loyal* to him and the company. To *look* for another job was unacceptable. To *take* another job was to be personally disloyal to him. Such a person became an outcast who was to be forgotten.

The man was a millionaire many times over. He had been born in humble circumstances and never went to high school. He worked and cared for his younger siblings and his mother. He and his wife never had children. He looked upon his employees as his children in adulthood after his siblings and mother became independent. The effect of his transferences of patriarchal needs to his employees made him a codependent for their addiction to the company and to him. Similar dependencies can be seen in other addictions, particularly to alcohol.

The tragedy of this story is that when the CEO died, the grief of the employees was profound. Soon the candy factory was closed and the property sold. All employees were out of a job. They had lost their "father" *and* their jobs within a year's time. I do not have firsthand information as to how they handled their grief. Many of them, I know, were at or near their retirement age, and could be cared for with retirement pay and the generous severance pay that his widow provided.

This story might be thought to be the opposite of the situation of corporations like Sears, IBM, Boeing, Philip Morris, Xerox, and General Electric. Not so fast! Employees at these companies fifteen years ago and into the present had many of the assumptions about their *depending* on "the company" for a lifetime job. Only a few of them had developed off duty hobbies that could easily be turned into a money-making situation. Five of them were what Corbin calls *indipreneurs* (a combination of the words independent and entrepreneur). By this, she means people who have enough independence to do well whether or not the company provided a job for them. They can grieve the loss of their job and fellowship with other employees, but the grief is not likely to become complicated or even pathological, because they have healthy independence toward the place and managers of the company for whom they work.

Conversely, the employer is wise to encourage employees to cultivate new skills and independence. To do so makes them more creative and innovative employees. This frees them from a lifetime dependency on the employer. The company functions in a corporate world where masses of people are discharged to cope with market downturns. This is called downsizing.

GRIEF AND SEPARATION IN CORPORATE DOWNSIZING

Corporate downsizing has become exceptionally prevalent in the contemporary work place. It has several dynamics. First, competition arises to challenge companies that previously had a corner on the market. For example Wal Mart has outdone K-Mart as a discount retailer. On September 8, 1994, ABC News carried the story that K-Mart was discharging six thousand employees and closing eleven of their large stores. Second, new technologies are invented that create machines that can do some of the workforce tasks. Third, many companies are multinational and can shift production to the place in the world where production can be done for less money. Fourth, poor decision making at the top of a company forces the shrinking of employment payrolls to offset losses caused by bad judgment in the management. Not all of this bad luck is caused by poor management. Managers retire or die, with the result that a whole new management sets about modernizing the entire corporation.

In any event, downsizing becomes necessary. For example, in 1993 the following companies experienced downsizing:[2]

Sears	50,000 layoffs
IBM	35,000 layoffs
Boeing	28,000 layoffs
Philip Morris	14,000 layoffs
Kodak	12,000 layoffs
Xerox	10,000 layoffs
General Electric	10,000 layoffs

This makes a total of layoffs of 159,000! Add to this the closings of military installations and the reduction-in-force of military personnel. Both civilian and military people are necessarily thrust into an intense grief situation. In the last year, I have had letters from two chaplains who hold the rank of colonel who are being separated from the army. Their efficiency ratings have been consistently excellent for the decades they have been in the army. Now, in civilian life, they must take positions in their denominations at an entry level. The redeeming feature is their retirement pay compensates considerably for the difference in income they receive from churches.

Then, too, denominations themselves are having to downsize. One denomination I know has had to lay off nearly four hundred persons in a very short while. Many took early retirement. Some were indipreneurial and have been able to establish self-employed work. Younger persons, however, must start a second career with some other organization or return to the pastorate, their "first love." Yet, they have to bear the grief and separation from their former colleagues on a daily basis.

All of these companies and institutions paid good to excellent salaries and wages. Those persons laid off quite often are forced to take jobs that pay much less. Persons taking lower paying jobs grieve at having to do so. It is a loss of status for them. More than this, they must downsize their personal standards of living. Every luxury must be trimmed. They are also grieved at having to break this news to their families.

One more source of stress, grief, including silent anger is that the employees who are *not* laid off may be asked to take over the duties of the persons laid off. I work in an agency that formerly had two secretaries for one unit. Both of them quit to take less oppressive jobs. One got another job that paid more. Now one secretary does the work that both had done before. This is known as the "stretch-out system." This was a déjà vu experience for me. When I was a child, my mother, a single parent, was a weaver in a cotton mill. One day she would have six looms to keep running and "side weave" with six. The next day, the side weaver had been laid off and my mother would have *twelve* looms to keep running. She would say, "I run my legs off and I can't keep up." In the treatment of our secretaries, I felt a sense of rage because I had first felt rage about the treatment of my mother in what was called "the stretch-out system."

MERGERS

Companies are merging with each other in order to survive. In some instances they merge in order to become conglomerates to exercise more power in the marketplace. The stress on employees involves some or all of them having to move locations from one place to another. This is one option. Another option is to leave the company because of the preference to remain in the location where they are because it is home to them and their nuclear and extended families. The ages of employees are factors in moving or staying. If the person is anywhere near retirement age he or she may opt for early retirement. Or he or she may have multiple skills and can get comparable employment without "going with the company."

Examples of mergers are in the business section of your newspaper or a copy of *The Wall Street Journal*. My morning paper of today tells of the speculation that the Columbia/Health Care of America hospital chain will move from its home office in Louisville to one of three other locations, although a spokeswoman for Columbia/Health Care Corporation "is not looking at any state. We have a commitment to Louisville." Background information is this. Columbia/HCA is a conglomerate of three hospital chains—Columbia, HCA, and Galen, the hospital chain formerly named Humana, a combined hospital and medical insurance company. When Columbia/HCA merged with Galen three or four years ago, they moved their headquarters to

Louisville. But Kentucky has leveled a two percent tax on hospitals, doctors, insurance companies, and drugstores. This is on their gross incomes, which cost, it seems, has been immediately passed on to the consumer. In spite of denials by Columbia/HCA the rumors of plans to move to another state persist.

It is inevitable that these rumors create in corporate employees anticipatory grief about job security or the possibility of having to move to another state. As Buono and Bowdich say: "At the extreme, people can become obsessed with the process, continually speculating about what it means for them personally. Estimates suggest that more than two hours of potentially productive work . . . time that is spent gossiping about the combination . . . .[or move]."[3] Managerial staff can do much to allay the anticipatory grief and anxiety by giving factual, consistent, honest messages to employees. Vague, inconsistent, and dishonest messages undermine management's credibility and employees support of the change in mergers and moving of headquarters to a distant place.

Dialogue and feedback sessions can go a long way toward enabling people to mourn the change. Pastoral groups in the church led by the pastor who understands grief can enable employees who are members of his or her parish to ventilate anger, rage, sadness, and fear of the unknown. Obviously the pastor cannot "represent" management, although I saw this happen in cotton mill communities when I was a teenager. To do so meant that the pastor was being "paid off" by the management, whether it was true or not.

Up to this point, this discussion has dealt with mergers and moving of secular companies. But mergers have occurred between denominations and denominational institutions such as literature publishers for use such as Sunday school and other materials. Mergers occur between religious book publishers, seminaries, and missionary boards, and so on. Grief reactions occur here just as in secular organizations.

For example, the two major Presbyterian bodies—Presbyterian Church (U.S.A.) and Presbyterian Church (U.S.)—have merged *and* changed the locations of both agencies to a third city. The Presbyterian (U.S.A.) moved from New York and Philadelphia and the Presbyterians (U.S.) moved from Atlanta. They both moved to Louisville, Kentucky. In addition to this the combined group has had to downsize because of shrinkage of financial support.

The two denominations each had a publishing house. Westminster

Press was in Philadelphia; John Knox Press was in Atlanta. Both moved to Louisville and merged into Westminster/John Knox Press. But in the ensuing years a major turnover has left a smaller number of largely new personnel. I have a deep affection for this press, because they have published many of my books since 1951. I have felt grief at the loss by resignation and retirement of friends. Relocation has been severe and grievous for many in the church generally and the press particularly. Imagine moving from New York's millions to Louisville's hundreds of thousands! I have just learned of one person who has returned to New York just as we had begun a friendship in work.

PASTORAL CARE IN RELATION TO MERGERS

The care of individuals and families facing and enduring mergers in the workplace is a difficult situation to focus and manage.

The first place to start is with families whose needs for basic housing, food, clothing, and so forth are not being met. Pride may keep them from letting anyone know. Many pastors have a great respect for and use of the grapevine, or the informal exchange of sensitive information. Intimate friends of such a family may tell the pastor of their plight. Also, hitherto very active members may cease to come to church altogether. If the family does not go to church at all, their neighbors may know of their situation and convey it to the parish pastor.

If, then, the situation is reliably known by the pastor, a strong initiative may be taken by visiting in their home. If basic needs can be identified, such as food and clothes, many churches have clothes closets and pantries established and replenished regularly by church members. Their children outgrow clothes that are not likely to be used again. Extra canned goods are bought and donated. These can be tactfully delivered to such a home. If the family is on the verge of losing their home, the church that has a committee for emergency help may devise and provide a transitional place for them to live.

Upper-middle and lower-upper class communities rarely present such needs. In upper-lower and lower-lower class communities these needs are not unusual at all. But more affluent churches can establish a sister church relationship with a less affluent church. Not only material needs can be shared, but spiritual needs as well. Such churches have many needs in common other than economic ones. For example, young people's music groups have much in common. Job centers for high school and college students in the spring can be shared. Even worship events are possible if pastors and lay leaders are committed to such sharing. Redistribution of wealth is a Christian as well as a political concern!

Another pastoral care approach to people squeezed out of jobs is possible when several or many families are in the same situation. Group discussions for ventilation of grief, anger, and desperation can be called together. Some of the sessions can be devoted to sharing information about reemployment opportunities and self-employment; indipreneurial efforts and brainstorming can be initiated to generate ideas for solving the problems created. These group approaches apply not only to casualties of mergers but also to those of downsizing, company closings, leveraged buyouts, and hostile takeovers.

But no substitute exists for the prior-to-the-crises personal relationship between a pastor and the person who is a casualty of these workplace events. A well built and maintained pastoral bond of friendship naturally goes into action when the person loses his or her job for any reason. A pastor is fortunate to "be there for them."

Seminaries also merge. Three seminaries—Colgate-Rochester in Rochester, New York; Crozer in Crozer, Pennsylvania, both of which are Baptist; and a very small Episcopal Seminary, Bexley-Hall, merged in 1970. The Crozer and Bexley Hall seminaries moved to Rochester as they merged with Colgate-Rochester Seminary. The advantage they gained was to be affiliated with a university. The merged organization is now named Colgate-Rochester-Bexley-Hall-Crozer Seminary.

But the moving forces that prompted the merger were, first, the exceptionally small faculty (four professors and a dean) and student body of Bexley Hall and, second, a severe financial crisis at Crozer. The reason for this crisis was an executive order in 1969 by President Nixon that grants and bequests to nonprofit institutions would be controlled by federal inspectors, effectively ending such sources of money for Crozer. Then Crozer made its move to Rochester.

I conversed with Edward Thornton of the Crozer faculty about the reactions to the move. He says that there were seventeen faculty members. Seven made the move to Rochester and ten did not (they got jobs elsewhere). He says that the morale of the school before this move was

exceptionally good. But, from his point of view, this is still the worst
grief of his life, worse even than the death of his parents in their very
advanced years. The dissolution of the Crozer faculty was like the end
of a Camelot for them. But the merger went smoothly as far as the qual-
ity of education and the freedom from conflict were concerned. Yet
personal grief and separation anxiety were a major stress.

The pastoral omission in these situations is that local pastors will
assume that seminary professors and their families can fend for themselves for pastoral care. But rituals of separation such as multiple family gatherings and luncheons with individuals, and special attention to
signs of clinical depression underneath the normal depression of grief
can be powerful channels of the care of the presence of God.

THE LEVERAGED BUYOUT

A company is at risk for being bought out. The leveraged buyout is one
kind of buyout. Here, the buyer uses as little cash as possible to do so.
He, she, or they may borrow the money to pay for the company. Or
they may use securities and bonds to do so. In the buyout the agreement may be naturally helpful and without conflict. But, it seems to
me, it must be a higher risk transaction as contracted with buy-outs
where large amounts of cash are used for the purchase. After the buyout the company bought by borrowed money is stable only as long as
the payments on the borrowed money are forthcoming, and the bonds
and securities are not shaky ones.

In any event, these takeovers, once accomplished, can shake up the
work force in unpredictable ways. Promotions and demotions, the
freezing of certain people's advancement by effort and seniority, the
replacement of personnel by the new owners' own people can occur
without prior notice.

The grief and separation caused by multiple frustrations are deeply
significant. A pastor can be a studious listener to employees; a pastor
can provide encouragement and letters of recommendation to other
jobs. He or she can give continuity of care as their persons move
through the collages of emotions—anxiety of the unknown, the shock
of being singled out as expendable by the new owners, and the anger
at the fact that life is unfair, depression, and so on.

THE HOSTILE TAKEOVER

In the secular business and industrial world a company can be taken over against the will and intentions of its owners. Political forces are used aggressively by the prospective but hostile owners. For example, lobbyists can influence state legislatures to pass or refuse to pass laws that facilitate the takeover of their companies. Anything goes! In the corporate world hostile takeovers occur both internally and from the outside of a corporation. For example, a company of health care cost containment was taken over from one partner owning 20 percent of the stock by another owning 80 percent. The conflict was finally settled after a five-month court battle that was settled out of court. Deception and betrayal motivated a man who had been trusted as a friend.

Several hostile takeover attempts have been made in the telecommunications field. There have been some external threats. Time Warner has been trying to acquire part of NBC. Ted Turner of CNN and affiliates "said that he wanted to buy NBC but that Time Warner, which owns about 20 percent of Turner Broadcasting's stock, blocked his efforts."[4]

Hostile takeovers in the corporate world are fueled by money and manipulation of stock. One stock owner, possibly joined together by other owners, overtly or covertly, buy up the majority of the company's stock. The next step is to take over the management of the company replacing other managers and production personnel. This is where much of the grief and separation occurs. Pastors may hear of this from another member of the church: "I think you would like to know. Some big upheavals in so and so's work are worrying him to death." A direct contact with the person is needed. One of the great traditional privileges of a pastor is to take full initiative toward people who are hurting. They may be too depressed—or ashamed—to take initiative toward us.

The medium of exchange in hostile takeovers is money—owned or borrowed. Subterfuge, deception, betrayal, and manipulation are prevalent. The only difference in an institutional takeover is that money is hidden discreetly. But essentially both corporate and institutional takeovers have the same ingredients. Ostensibly, though, another difference exists in that colleges, universities, and seminaries operate on the spoken agenda by means of political power through organization and the use of trustees of a given ideological bent. Mix all these together in a religious denomination and its institutions and you have unairconditioned misery coming from the south end of hell.

But the main focus of our concern is ministering to separated, alienated, and bereaved persons whose lives have been completely disorganized by the changes created in the personnel of a corporation or institution.

I am most familiar with the hostile takeovers in the ecclesiastical world of institutions, especially seminaries and colleges. Here I am more than a reader or hearing witness of the trauma.

One of the earlier hostile takeovers of a religious institution occurred in the 1970s when Jacob Preus led a battle over the theological position of the Missouri Synod's Concordia Seminary in St. Louis. Preus and other literalist inerrantist Bible believers took over the school. He was president of the Synod in 1969–1981 and caused a split that led some 200 congregations and more than a 100,000 members to leave the denomination, while some 45 teachers and 400 students left to form a seminary in exile."[5] Preus died on August 13, 1994 while visiting his daughter and son-in-law in Minneapolis. His home was in St. Louis.

   Hostile takeovers are no new things to ecclesiastical denominations, especially within denominations. Conflict today is not between but within denominations. The conflict is usually a blend of ideology and power. The targets of the takeovers are book publishing houses, denominational literature publishing houses, and colleges, universities, and theological seminaries.

A long conflict has been raging between contending ideological leaders in the Southern Baptist Convention. In 1979 a group of fundamentalists announced their intention to take over the leadership of the convention. The method of doing so was to elect fundamentalist presidents of the convention to the two-year terms of each president. The president had the sole power to appoint members to the Committee on Boards and Committees. In turn, this committee appointed replacements for boards and committees of agencies of the institutions of the convention, such as the Sunday School Board, the Foreign Mission Board, the Executive Committee, the Christian Life Commission, the Education Commission, the six seminaries, and so on. As "moderate" members of their agencies rotated off the boards of trustees of these agencies, they were regularly replaced by "fundamentalists." These moves have been orchestrated by a small group of political strategists who have kept the process alive and supervised it. The process of the takeover has been completed at the national level. Three of the major seminaries—Southeastern Theological Seminary in Wake Forest, North Carolina; The Southern Baptist Theological Seminary in Louisville, Kentucky; and Southwestern Theological Seminary in Fort Worth, Texas have been taken over by extremist boards of trustees and presidents. I will describe what happened in one of these.

The Southern Baptist Theological Seminary

The Southern Baptist Theological Seminary in Louisville, Kentucky, was the second theological school to be taken over in a hostile way by Southern Baptist fundamentalists. The trustee board was taken over by fundamentalists in 1991. It is now completely composed of politically minded fundamentalists. Not all fundamentalists are politically organized in a takeover pattern of action. Those who are have a very explicit agenda. That agenda is somewhat as follows:

1. The belief in the literal, inerrant Bible. All parts of the Bible are equally inspired.

2. A pro-life opposition to abortion with little or no discussion of possible differences between abortions or discussion of extenuating circumstances of some cases.

3. Opposition to women's ordination to the ministry, and antifeminist belief such as the submission of women to men. One convention-passed resolution says women are the initiators of sin in Eve's response to temptation.

4. Extreme opposition to all different kinds of homosexuality.

5. The primary authority of the pastor over the congregation.

6. The ideal of a *Christian* America as evidenced in the Christian Coalition's effort to take over control of school boards, other local candidates as well as members of the state legislatures, the national House of Representatives and Senate.

7. A fundamentalist takeover of psychiatry by doctors who are fundamentalists.[6]

The takeover of the membership of the trustees of The Southern

Baptist Theological Seminary occurred in 1993. The takeover of the administration of the school came upon the retirement of the moderate president, Roy Lee Honeycutt, in 1993. He was replaced by a fundamentalist, Albert Mohler, in the same year. Between 1990 and 1994, forty-four of seventy-five faculty members resigned or retired. One faculty member, a professor of Christian Ethics, was forced into early retirement because of his belief and teachings about the rights of women to legal abortions. In August 1994, Molly Marshall, a moderate associate professor with tenure, was forced to resign or be fired because the administration "had the votes" (among trustees) to do so. She was the only woman at the time with tenure on the School of Theology faculty. At this time of writing (September 23, 1994), the faculty is in an overwhelming opposition to the president of the school. The story is an ongoing saga of bereavement over the loss of long-term friendships and colleagueships of faculty members. Some remaining faculty members are near retirement. In the course of the takeover process, anger, depression, physical illness, and death of three faculty members from heart attacks or cancer are the form of grief and separation that has been the lot of faculty members.

One form of recovery of the faculty of the dispersion is to stay in touch by telephone, or visiting each other. "War stories" are retold, but more positively stories about each other's new work; books published, and families' new adventures are shared. Another is staying in touch by letter, telephone, and visits with their graduate supervising professors with whom they later taught. These persons serve as pastors in a very real sense of the word by reason of having been mentors and having become colleagues and friends, and by being family members in the family of God. A more humorous pastime is "fundamentalist bird watchers" equipped with powerful binoculars, that work even in night and fog. Withdrawing from such situations is prescribed in 1 Timothy 6:1-10!

VIOLENCE IN THE WORKPLACE

"Murder has become the number one cause of death for women in the workplace; for men it is third, after machine related mishaps and driving accidents. Today more than 100 American are murdered on the job, 32 percent more than the annual averages in the '80s."[7]

These figures take on very personal dimensions when specific instances and people are mentioned. For example, an April 21, 1994 Ladislar Antalik, 38, after having quit his job at Sumitomo Electric Fiber Optics Corporation, returned to the company and turned the place into a bloody mess. Again, Auburn Calloway attacked three of his fellow Federal Express pilots while in flight. The next day he was scheduled to face a disciplinary hearing that he had lied about his military and work experience.[8]

Nearer to my home, on September 14, 1989, Joseph Wesbecker, who had been put on disability for mental illness, returned to Standard Gravure with an AK-47 and either killed or wounded 20 people. Then he killed himself. He was being treated with the antidepressant Prozac. The survivors of those murdered and those disabled are now, five years later, suing Eli Lilly, the manufacturer of the drug Prozac.

At Fort Knox Army Base, 35 miles from Louisville, on October 18, 1993 a disgruntled employee returned to the workplace and killed three employees and wounded two more before killing himself. Now the survivors are demanding an explanation of the tragedy. As one said, "I want some explanation (for) why he was never charged, and what they are going to do." The man was buried with full military honors. The two wounded and disabled people, their families, and the bereaved families of those killed want some answers from the Army.[9]

These bereavements after such slaughters are sudden, and traumatic, and recovery is very complicated. Survivors are stuck in anger and have major difficulties in moving through their grief.

Such killings leave survivors not only of family members but of fellow workers. Many have post-traumatic stress syndrome, which involves repeated flashbacks. Hostility to their employers is not an unusual part of the grief process.

Pastoral care in such situations should include getting to the scene of the tragedy as soon as is possible. If a parishioner is one of the casualties, then getting to the person, although it is a task filled with confusion, is imperative. Continuity of care must be given. The anniversary of the event can be remembered with visits, telephone calls, and letters. The senselessness of the death will remain a mystery to the survivors. The quest for persons to blame continues.

The grief in cases of violence is a communal grief. Reunions of survivors may occur. Being a pastoral presence at such reunions brings the presence of God to the occasions, a reminder of the participant's own mortality and hope in Jesus Christ. After all, he was executed in his workplace, too. They are not alone. The grief of families of people murdered in the workplace is not merely sudden. It extends over years of chronic sorrow and may move into a litigation phase. Pastoral care in these situations involves several different pastors. Coordinating the work of different pastors is important.

Furthermore, attention needs to be given at the individual and family level of pastoral care to the *family of the perpetrators.* Several instances of these mass murders included the suicide of the perpetrator. Rarely is public condolence extended to these families. In addition to their private grief, they have the omnipresent noses of the media complicating their grief. One wonders what ordered attention in prayer in churches is given to these families.

The corporate assurance of the whole congregation is a source of help in time of need. "Suffering produces endurance; endurance produces character; character produces hope; and hope does not disappoint us, because God's love has been poured into our hearts by the Holy Spirit" (Rom. 5:5).

6

GRIEF AND SEPARATION IN THE LIFE OF FAITH IN JESUS CHRIST

Both we as pastors and those in grief and separation to whom we minister do so before God and in God's presence, whether we know it or not. Routinely, God is the target of much anger in times of grief and separation. Remarkably enough, rarely do we hear anger directed at Jesus Christ. It is directed toward a God who is vindictive and punitive, who causes death and traumatic separations such as the divorce of spouses or alienation of children from parents. For example, a patient in a hospital asked me, "Why did God kill my baby?" I asked her, "Do you think Jesus would kill your baby?" She said that she did not, because Jesus loved little children. We have seen the light of the knowledge of God in the face of Jesus Christ (2 Cor. 4:6). To think of God apart from Jesus Christ strikes terror in our hearts because we see a God for whom we blame for all adversity, chaos, destruction, and punishment. The God and Father of our Lord Jesus Christ, the Father of mercies and the God of all comfort, is just the opposite.

Grief and separation in the life of faith in Jesus Christ is the crux of our conversation in this book. Let us fix our gaze on him.

Jesus faced death himself. Over the last three years of his public ministry death hung over his head as the consequence of his challenge of the foundations of the religious plurocracy of his time. In his ministry to Lazarus, Martha, and Mary, he heard from a distance that Lazarus was ill. In spite of his personal danger of being stoned by the Jews, he went back into Judea to visit Lazarus, Martha, and Mary, all of whom he loved. His disciples thought Lazarus was asleep, but Jesus said plainly, "Lazarus is dead" (John 11:14). He met with Martha and Mary and wept with them in shared grief. He prayed to God the Father, thanking God that he always heard him. Then he called in a loud voice to Lazarus in his tomb: "Lazarus, come out" (John 11:43). Lazarus came out alive.

Again, he was asked by Jairus to come to his daughter who he thought was dying. On his way he healed the woman with a flow of blood. As she touched his garment she was healed. He continued to Jairus's home. He told those weeping around Jairus's daughter that she was not dead but sleeping. One supposes that she was as we say today in a deep coma. This caused the others to laugh. In the face of their laughter, Jesus "took her by the hand and said, 'Child arise,'" and she got up at once, and he directed that something should be given to her to eat" (Luke 8:53-55).

It seems Jesus never attended a funeral but always a resurrection or a renewal of life. Yet deaths occurred all around him. He was aware of the Galileans upon whom the Tower of Siloam fell and eighteen men were killed (Luke 13:4). He saw children in the marketplace playing funeral (Luke 8:31). And as he entered Gethsemane, he told his disciples, "My soul is very sorrowful even to death; remain here and watch with me" (Matt. 26:38).

Then he was sadistically murdered by the Roman army on a cross. As he was dying he uttered the cry of human dereliction, "My God, My God, why have you forsaken me?" the ultimate in grief and separation. It took God three days to answer him with his resurrection from the dead. He triumphed over death. In him death itself was dead.

FAITH IN CHRIST IN GRIEF AND SEPARATION

This journey of Jesus Christ provides the way of life we are to live in the face of grief and separation. The Apostle Paul made this clear. We recapitulate Jesus' experience throughout our lives. Paul says, "I have been crucified with Christ; it is no longer I who live, but Christ who lives in me; and the life I now live in the flesh I live by faith in the Son of God who loved me and gave himself for me" (Gal. 2:20).

Paul commends this to us as a way of life: "Do you not know that all of us who have been baptized into Christ were baptized into his death? We were buried with him in baptism into death, so that as Christ was raised from the dead by the glory of his Father, we too may walk in the newness of life" (Rom. 6:3-4).

When we are bereaved—whether from the loss of someone by death or by separation—we go with them through a death of an old life, through a burial of that life, and to a resurrection to a new life.

I was talking with my pastor last week about his six-year-old son. They were riding in the car. The child said to his father, "I don't want to grow up. Can you make me three years old again?" His father said, "No, I can't do that. Do you mean school is not so good?" His son said, "Yes. And you can't make me three again." The father said, "No. Those days are gone. But new, good days are ahead."

We all have much in common with that child. At each transition in the life cycle we die to the era just past. We are separated. We go through a transition. We are reunited in a new life. Human life moves forward or regresses in the face of the crises of growth with which the life cycle presents us. A whole series of researchers have almost with one voice described the ways in which we grow by leaving place and finding a new station in life.[1] This seems to be the very nature of human existence itself.

The death, burial, and resurrection of Jesus represents his separation, transition, and reunion with us. When we are separated—as in divorce or death or a new cycle of life such as retirement—old things pass away. There is a time of mourning and transition. If we do not regress into nostalgia for the past, we move forward to a reunion with a new life.

THE LEAP OF FAITH

This moving forward is not an automatic, foreordained necessity. It takes place when we are given by God the courage to make the leap of faith it takes to move from one stage to the other. Paul describes the leap in detail in Romans 5:3-5: "Suffering produces endurance, endurance produces character, and character produces hope, and hope does not disappoint us, because God's love has been poured into our hearts through the Holy Spirit which has been given us."

This hope amounts to being empowered by the Spirit of God to face life with courage. This courage gives us the strength to take the "leap of faith" into the unknown.

In the experience of the loss of someone by death, the death itself has rites of separation—the visitation of friends, the sharing of food, and in some instances the wake. These do not require a leap of faith because the bereaved is surrounded by others who support him or her which he or she simply receives passively.

The rituals of transition demand more courage in facing returning home without the loved one, disposing of his or her personal effects, answering letters of condolence, putting the finances in order. These chores take energy that grief depletes at the same time. Hopefully, there are sons and daughters of encouragement—they may be friends and relatives who put heart into the bereaved to get these things done. All in all, though, this is almost a time of limbo when courage is at low ebb.

In the rituals of reunion with life as it moves ahead, a real leap of faith is required. This is the resurrection to a new life. It is the time of the courage to leave the mourning behind and to enter the gates of a new life.

THE LIFE OF FAITH IN THE LIFE CYCLE

My pastor's six-year-old son's insight about wanting to be three years old is prophetic of all of the separations, transitions, and reunions of the rest of his life. Growth requires the courage to be at each new era of life and the courage to take the leap of faith into each new era of life. If we look on separations that occur at each new era of the life cycle as calling for this kind of courage then the experience of dying from an old era and being born into a new existence brings with it both pain and joy, both a kind of death and a kind of resurrection. If we focus these experiences on the presence of the living Christ, we are never alone.

PASTORAL LEADERSHIP

As children are born, as they start to school, as they are baptized, as they graduate from high school or college, as they join the workforce, as they get married, as they in too many circumstances get divorced, as they lose jobs, as they have children (and the cycle begins anew with their children), as they become ill or have disabling accidents, as they retire, as they lose a mate by death, as they face death themselves—we as pastors are, at our best, continuity persons, fellow pilgrims. John Bunyan, in *Pilgrim's Progress* has a character Mr. Greatheart who, like Barnabas was, is a person of encouragement. The crises of grief and separation are troubled waters. We are "bridges over troubled waters." Yet on every bridge with any traffic is a "No Parking" sign. Others are coming after you! Keep moving! In the journey of the soul, the life of faith in Jesus Christ, we keep people moving forward. We as pastors encourage and nurture this forward movement at times of grief and separation. We discourage shrinking back or simply parking where one is. As Hebrews 10:38-39 puts it:

"'My righteous one shall live by faith, and if he shrinks back my soul has no pleasure in him.' But we are not of those who shrink back and are destroyed, but of those who have faith and keep their souls."

NOTES

Chapter 2

1. More extensive discussion of them can by found in *The Meaning of Human Suffering*, ed. Flavian Dougherty, C.P. (New Youth: Human Sciences Press, 1982). In the volume I wrote chapter 6, "Forms of Grief: Diagnosis, Meaning, and Treatment." This study was popularized with a pastoral care handbook for suffering persons, *Your Particular Grief* (Louisville: Westminster/John Knox, 1981).
   2. *A Treasury of Great Poems*, ed. Louis Untermeyer (New York: Simon and Schuster, 1955), pp. 876–77.
   3. (Macon, GA: Smyth and Helwys Publishing, Inc., 1993).
   4. Helen Rosen, *Unspoken Grief: Coping with Childhood Sibling Loss* (Lexington, Mass.: D.C. Health and Company, 1986), p. 38.
   5. Mary Ann Sweeney, John E. Baker, and Esther Bross, "'The Story' of a Death," *Journal of Marital and Family Therapy*, 20 (July, 1994), 3: 288.
   6. Ibid., 289–90.
   7. Ibid., 291.
   8. Bruce Metzger and Michael Coogan, *New Oxford Companion to the Bible* (New York: Oxford University Press, 1993), p. 798.

Chapter 3

1 *A Treasury of Great Poems*, ed. Louis Untermeyer (New York: Simon and Schuster, 1955), p. 655.
   2. Otto Rank, *Will Therapy and Truth & Reality* (New York: Alfred A. Knopf, 1945), p. 124.
   3. Otto Rank, *The Trauma of Birth* (New York: Robert Brunner, 1952), p. 5.
   4. Erik Erikson, *Identity and the Life Cycle* (New York: International Universities Press, 1959), pp. 55–56.
   5. James Agee, *A Death in the Family* (New York: Bantam Books, 1969),p. 237.

6. Rosen, *Unspoken Grief*, p. 27.
7. Rosen, *Unspoken Grief*, pp. 167–168.
8. *Separation and Depression*, ed. John P. Scott and Edward Seary (New York: American Association for the Advancement of Science, Pub. No. 24, 1973), pp. 215 ff.
9. See also my book *Managing Your Stress* (Minneapolis: Augsburg Publishing House, 1983).
10. Velma Stevens, *Grief Work* (Nashville: Broadman Press, 1990), pp. 17–18.
11. C. S. Lewis, *A Grief Observed* (New York: Bantam Press, 1976).
12. Ibid., 147.
13 Ibid., 148.
14. Ibid., 48–49
15. Ibid., 60.
16. Beverly Raphael, *The Anatomy of Bereavement* (New York: Basic Books, 1983), p. 229.
17. Ibid., 236.
18. Ibid., 239.
19. William Amos, *When AIDS Comes to Church* (Louisville: Westminster/John Knox, 1988).
20. William Masters, Virginia Johnson, and Robert Kolodny, *On Sex and Human Loving* (Boston: Little Brown and Co., 1988), p. 181.
21. *Merck's Manual of Diagnosis and Therapy*, (Rahway, New Jersey: Merck, Sharpe, and Dohme Laboratories, published in updated form periodically).
22. John Hewett, *After Suicide* (Louisville: Westminster/John Knox, 1980).
23. Wayne E. Oates, *Pastor's Handbook*, (Louisville: Westminster/John Knox Press, 1980). Volume 1, chapter 4, pp. 73–87.

Chapter 4

1. "The Foreigner Within Us," The *Christian Science Monitor* 7 August, 1991, p. 23.
2. "The Marriage Contract," In *Progress in Group and Family Therapy*, eds. Clifford Sager, and Helen Kaplan (New York: Brunner/Mazel, Inc., 1972), pp. 483–497.
3. Ibid.
4. *Divorce and Second Marriage* (New York: The Seabury Press, 1983), p. 39.

Chapter 5

1. Carolyn Corbin, *Conquering Corporate Codependence* (Englewood Cliffs, New Jersey: Prentice Hall, 1993), p. 8.
2. "Bumstead, You're Down-Sized," *Time*, 18 April 1994, 22.
3. Anthony Buono and James L. Bowdich, *The Human Side of Mergers and Acquisitions* (San Francisco: Jossey-Bass, Inc., 1989), p. 117.

4. *The Wall Street Journal*. 76, 244, 28 September 1994, 1, 3.

5. "Lutheran Leader Preus Dies," *Christian Century*, Vol. 111, August 24–31, 1994, 777–78.

6. See Frank B. Minirth and Walter Byrd, *Christian Psychiatry*, rev. and ex. ed. (Old Tappan, New Jersey: Fleming H. Revell Co., 1977) and R.S. McGee, *In Search of Significance* (Waco, Texas: Word Books, 1990).

7. *Time*, 24 April 1994, 35–36.

8. Ibid., 36.

9. "Families Want Army to Explain Slayings," Louisville *Courier Journal*, 26 September 1994, A–1.

Chapter 6

1. Beginning with Arnold Van Genneys in his book, *The Rites of Passage*; Paul Radin, *Primitive Religion*; Louis Sherrill, *The Struggle of the Soul*; Gail Sheehy, *Passages*; Erik Erikson, and many others

FURTHER READING

I. BOOKS FOR THE PASTOR

Buono, Anthony F., and James L. Bowditch. *The Human Side of Mergers and Acquisitions.* San Francisco: Jossey-Bass, Inc., 1989.

Bowlby, John. *Attachment and Loss: Sadness and Depression.* Vol. 3. New York: Basic Books, 1982.

Corbin, Carolyn. *Conquering Corporate Co-Dependence.* Englewood Cliffs, New Jersey: Prentice-Hall, 1993.

Deal, Terence E., and Allen Kennedy. *Corporate Cultures: The Rites and Rituals of Corporate Life.* Reading, Mass.: Addison-Wesley Publishing Co., 1983.

Erikson, Erik. *Identity and the Life Cycle.* New York: International Press, 1959.

Gerkin, Charles W. *Crisis Experience in Modern Life.* Nashville:Abingdon Press, 1979.

Harbough, Gary L. *The Pastor as Person.* Minneapolis: Augsburg Publishing House, 1984.

Kübler-Ross, Elisabeth. *Death and Dying.* New York: Macmillan, 1989.

Lester, Andrew D. *Pastoral Care with Children in Times of Crisis.* Louisville: Westminster/John Knox, 1985.

Lifton, Robert. "Apathy and Numbing." In *The Meaning of Human Suffering.* Edited by Flavian Dougherty. New York: Science Press, 1982.

Merck's Manual of Diagnosis and Therapy. Edited by Robert Berkow,

M.D. Rahway, New Jersey: Merck, Sharpe, and Dohme (published periodically and updated).

Oates, Wayne E. *The Christian Pastor*. Third Edition. Louisville: Westminster/John Knox, 1982.

Rambo, Therese. *Treatment of Complicated Grief*. Champaign, Illinois: Research Press, 1993.

Rank, Otto. *Will Therapy and Truth and Reality*. New York: Alfred A. Knopf, 1945.

Raphael, B. *The Anatomy of Bereavement*. New York: Basic Books, 1983.

Rosen, Helen. *Unspoken Grief: Coping with Childhood Sibling Loss*. Lexington, Mass.: D. C. Heath and Co., 1986.

Sager, Clifford, Helen Kaplan, *et al*. "The Marriage Contract." In *Progress in Group Therapy*. Edited by Clifford Sager and Helen Kaplan. New York: Brunner/Mazel, 1972.

Separation and Depression. Edited by John P. Scott and Edward Seary. New York: American Association for the Advancement of Science. Pub. No. 24, 1973.

Sweeney, Mary Ann, John E. Baker, and Esther Bross. "'The Story' of a Death." *Journal of Marriage and Family Therapy*. 20 (July, 1994), 3: 287–300.

Switzer, David. *The Minister as Crisis Counselor*. Rev. ed. Nashville: Abingdon Press, 1986.

Waller, Willard and Reuben Hill. *The Family: A Dynamic Interpretation*. New York: Dryden Press, 1951.

II. BOOKS FOR LAYPERSONS AND PASTORS

Agee, James. *A Death in the Family*. New York: Bantam Books, 1969.

Amos, William. *When AIDS Comes to Church*. Westminster/John Knox, 1993.

Browning, Robert. "Prospice." In *A Treasury of Great Poems*. Edited by Louis Untermeyer. New York: Simon Schuster, Inc., 1955.

Bugg, Charles B. *Learning to Dream Again: From Grief to Gratitude*. Macon, Georgia: Smyth and Helwys Publishing Co., 1993.

Clemons, Hardy. *Saying Goodbye to Your Grief*. Macon, Georgia: Smyth and Helwys Publishing Co., 1984.